Sven Felix Kellerh

BERLIN

UNDER THE SWASTIKA

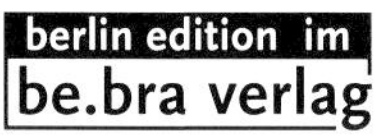

Also available as an ebook.

Bibliografische Information der Deutschen Bibliothek
Die Deutsche Bibliothek verzeichnet diese Publikation in der Deutschen Nationalbibliografie; detaillierte bibliografische Daten sind im Internet über http://dnb.ddb.de abrufbar.

Revised Edition

Berlin-Brandenburg, 2014
KulturBrauerei Haus 2
Schönhauser Allee 37, 10435 Berlin
post@bebraverlag.de
Translation: Penny Croucher, London
Layout: typegerecht berlin
Typesetting: Deepdene 10/13,5 pt
All photographs from bpk – Bildagentur für Kunst, Kultur und Geschichte
Cover picture: mauritius images / United Archives
Printed and bound by: Finidr, Český Těšín
ISBN 978-3-8148-0155-1 (print)
ISBN 978-3-8393-4113-1 (ebook)

www.bebraverlag.de

Contents

Berliners enthusiastically salute the Olympic Torch as it is carried through the German capital in the summer of 1936.

Prologue

The rows of uniformed men carrying flaming torches from the Tiergarten towards the Brandenburg Gate seem to be unending. They parade through the three most southerly of the five arches with their decorated columns and then march onwards around the small roadworks in front of the main archway. Watched by countless spectators the torch bearers continue across Pariser Platz and turn south at the first crossroads into Wilhelmstrasse, the street lined with government buildings. They march past the numerous German State ministries until they finally reach the Reich Chancellery opposite Wilhelmsplatz. (Reich = area under German rule. It literally means "realm" or "empire", but this is misleading because the monarchy no longer existed as the Kaiser ["Emporer"] had abdicated.) There, at the window of his office on the first floor, stands the newly elected Reich Chancellor of Germany: Adolf Hitler, leader of the National Socialist Party of German Workers (NSDAP) which has just won the majority of seats Reichstag (the German parliament). The "Führer" (= leader, head of State) salutes the thousands of men who are marching through the cold winter in his honour. It is many decades since the old victory arch of the Hohenzollern dynasty and the surrounding streets full of government buildings have witnessed such a triumphant procession as this on Monday evening 30th January 1933.

Even Hitler is overwhelmed by the enthusiasm which greets him. He asks his photographer, Heinrich Hoffmann: "Where has Goebbels managed to get hold of so many torches in such a short space of time?" Indeed the NSDAP Gauleiter of Berlin, experienced as he is in masterminding impressive backdrops for his "Führer", has surpassed even himself on this afternoon. It was not until just before 5 p.m. that the new Minister for the Interior, National Socialist Wilhlem Frick, lifted the ban that had existed on holding demonstrations at the Brandenburg Gate. Just two hours later all the members of the SA, the NSDAP and other Hitler sympathisers who heard Goebbels' rallying call, gather at the Kleiner Stern in the Tiergarten, the junction of Bellevueallee and Charlottenburger Chaussee. Torches are handed out, marching and brass bands set up the beat and soon tens of thousands of boots are hitting the asphalt in perfect time. At about 8.30 p.m. the front of the procession reaches its destination, the Reich Chancellery. The whole march past takes over three hours and the

The first re-enactment of the torchlight procession for the film "SA-Mann Brand".

Even the most well-known picture of the march through the Brandenburg Gate was not taken at the time but staged at a later date.

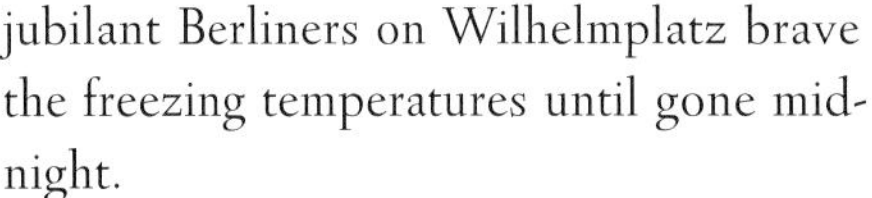

jubilant Berliners on Wilhelmplatz brave the freezing temperatures until gone midnight.

Goebbels, who on this evening makes his first radio broadcast ever, goes into raptures: "It is so moving for me to see how, in this city where we began six years ago with only a handful of people, the whole population is rising up and how they are all marching past; workers, citizens, farmers, students and soldiers – a great national community." On the same night he writes in his diary: "Endless. A million people on the move. The old man (Reich President Paul von Hindenburg) takes the salute. In the next building is Hitler. It is a new era! A spontaneous explosion of the people. Indescribable. More and more crowds." The British Ambassador, who also sees the marching columns from his Embassy in Wilhelmstrasse, gives a more truthful account of the events. Sir Horace Rumbold reports back to the Foreign Minister in London. "The Nazi press maintain that about half a million people took part in the torch procession, evidently without knowing that to complete such a parade it would have taken one hour for 10,000 men marching in lines of six and that for four hours 50,000 is the maximum number possible."

Quite apart from the question of numbers the few original photos of the torch procession are disappointing – underexposed and out of focus or blurred. There are no moving pictures at all. So, in the weeks that follow, the resourceful and unscrupulous Goebbels stages the torchlight procession twice more for the lenses of picture journalists and cameramen: once for the propaganda film "SA man Brand" and then, on an even larger scale, for the production of "Hans Westmar", also a feature film about the victory of National Socialism in Germany. Most of the photographs and all the film shots depicting the torchlight procession through the Brandenburg Gate come from these two staged versions of the parade. Right from the very start the new regime is based on lies and deception.

Democratically minded Berliners do not celebrate on 30th January 1933, the good feeling they had enjoyed on the occasion of the traditional Press Ball two days earlier has evaporated. The pacifist and Hitler

The torchlight procession on 30th January. This photo is authentic; there is a small roadworks which the procession has to march round.

opponent, Harry Graf Kessler writes with horror in his diary: "Today Berlin is in carnival mood. SA and SS troops and other steel helmets in uniform fill the streets, spectators cram the pavements. (...) The whole of Wilhelmsplatz is teeming with gaping crowds." Theodor Eschenburg, an employee of a large business concern, hears the radio coverage of the torchlight procession at an evening function in the exclusive home of one of his company directors. As they listen, the assembled company, all of a conservative persuasion, become increasingly dumbstruck. The 28 year old Eschenburg interrupts the silence with the question, "When will we be rid of Hitler again?" Max Liebermann, the Berlin artist, who lives in a building right next to the Brandenburg gate, expresses his feelings on this evening very succinctly: "It makes me want to vomit – but I couldn't stuff enough food down my throat." The darkest epoch in the history of the German capital begins with the torchlight procession through the Brandenburg Gate on 30th January 1933. This evening unleashes the indescribable violence which starts in Germany, spreads through Europe and eventually has consequences for the whole world. Millions upon millions of people lose their lives because of National Socialism and Hilter's war destroys so many cultural and economic values. Six decades later, the traces of twelve years of Nazi dictatorship from 1933 until 1945 are still evident – even if the divisions in Berlin, Germany and Europe have been overcome.

The Path to Power

On foreign soil

Adolf Hitler had his first experience of politics in Upper Bavaria, especially in the beer cellars of Munich and this was where his speeches, with their mixture of anti-Semitism and nationalist prejudice, were best received. In Berlin, by contrast, the National Socialists, founded in 1919 as the "German Workers' Party", enjoyed very little popularity and at first attracted no more than a few hundred supporters. Neither was there any enthusiasm for the exaggeratedly hate-ridden and hectoring speeches of the Nazi leader.

For Hitler Berlin was always a target in both senses of the word; both as an object of hatred and of desire, at the same time a measure of what he despised and yet his own personal "Promised Land". Since his four brief visits to Berlin as a soldier after the First World War, Hitler's relationship with the capital had been characterised by deep division. On the one hand his world view included the rejection of modern city life but on the other hand he was fascinated by the workings of a metropolis and by Berlin in particular. This contradiction is revealed in Hitler's "Mein Kampf", a confused book written in 1924-25 which is mainly a montage of stereotypes. At one point in the book the leader of the National Socialists attacks the city as a "merely a collection of blocks of flats and nothing more. It is difficult to see how a special attachment is to develop with such a meaningless place." Yet only a hundred pages on he writes: "The geopolitical significance of such a centrally situated city cannot be underestimated. A political movement can only gain long-term power by being part of the aura of a place suffused with the magical charm of a Mecca or Rome, and has as its substance an inner unity and pays homage to the summit of this unity." Despite all his criticism of modern cities Hitler had realised very early on that winning the political battle for Berlin would be decisive in the acquisition of power in and over Germany and for this reason, from 1920 onwards, he kept returning to the capital, sometimes for weeks at a time.

Some of his most important financial supporters lived here. His party was always hard up and constantly needed funds, not only because their leader was unemployed but also because they were producing a newspaper, the Völkische Beobachter (People's Observer), which ran at a loss. Hitler's first base in Berlin was the city home of the

A demonstration by a small group of Hitler supporters in November 1925 in the Lustgarten. In the background are the Berlin City Palace on the left and the City Command Headquarters on the right.

piano manufacturer Edwin Bechstein who lived near Museumsinsel (Museum Island). In these early years Bechstein's wife Helene was one of the NSDAP's most generous donors. She enjoyed entertaining Hitler and his "national" friends and sometimes even pawned jewellery or paintings to help out the charismatic bohemian from Munich. The Bechsteins' house at number six Johannisstrasse in central Berlin, which Hitler's confidant from those days Ernst Hanfstaengel jealously and condescendingly called "one of the grandest boxes in the inner city", was destroyed in the "Battle for Berlin" at the end of April 1945.

It was another sponsor who organised Hitler's first political appearance in Berlin. The former Director of Siemens, Emil Gansser, invited his protégé to the elegant "National Club", where he was to address the "inner circle" of senior officers, officials and businessmen and Hitler made his first speech there at the end of May 1922. The "National Club" was situated directly opposite the eastern entrance of the Reichstag; on this site today stands the Jakob-Kaiser-Haus, a parliamentary office building. Hitler's words evidently attracted interest as he was asked back for a repeat performance on 5 June 1922, but they failed to have any political effect and in spite of the (short-lived) support from the Berlin industrial baron Ernst von Borsig not enough money was raised to fund the NSDAP in Berlin.

The SA march through Berlin in 1930 under the protection of the police.

However, a few months later a Berlin group of the Munich splinter party emerged under the name of "Grossdeutsche Arbeiterpartei" (Workers' Party of Greater Germany), but they were unable to increase their membership to much more than their original 194 founder members, mainly because the democratically inclined Prussian Police rigorously and cleverly prevented any attempts by the right-wing extremists to get round the Prussia wide ban on the NSDAP which came into force on 15 November 1922. Throughout 1923 the Nazis remained insignificant in the capital. When Hitler called for a "march on Berlin" after the Munich Putsch on 8 November, there was only a small band of about 10 faithful followers who were ready to support the "coup d'état" – not a very impressive fighting force to conquer a city of millions.

Thanks to sympathetic judges in Bavaria, Hitler only had to serve one fifth of his already short sentence for high treason. By the end of 1924 he was free again and his first long journey took him back to Berlin. The German capital was clearly his most important destination outside Munich – as it had been between 1920 and 1923. In mid-March 1925, only two weeks after the lifting of the ban and the subsequent founding of a nationwide NSDAP, he met up with other politicians from the extreme right. This particular visit to Berlin is noteworthy because the talks were held in the Reichstag building in which, according to the accounts written by his own party, the Nazi "Führer" claimed never to have set foot before 1933. The insignificance of the NSDAP at this time can be demonstrated by the results of the first ballot in the Reich

Presidential election on 29 March 1925 when World War I General Erich Ludendorff, the candidate supported among others by Hitler, gained just 1.1% of the votes overall and as little as 0.4% in Berlin. Even more shattering was the result of the first election in which Hitler's Party took part; in 1925 in the local elections in Berlin the NSDAP polled 137 votes in Spandau, the only borough where they had a candidate. The official records list this as last place.

Berlins NSDAP Gauleiter (District Leader) Joseph Goebbels giving one of his typical speeches from an open car.

"Battle for Berlin"

Hitler wanted to change all this, but he still lacked both real support and the means to mobilise new party members. There had been a local Berlin NSDAP since February 1925 but initially they only attracted attention because of mismanagement and internal strife. In the first 18 months the Berlin NSDAP had to move offices several times, apparently because they could not pay even modest rents. From 1st August 1926 onwards the Party "resided" in some damp, dilapidated rooms on the ground floor of a building in the back courtyard of 109, Potsdamer Strasse between Pohl- and Lützowstrasse. The original building, which the several hundred Party members used to derisively call (among other things) the "Opium Den", has been destroyed and replaced with a new construction. Although the Berlin NSDAP was still small it quickly divided into two opposing wings. On one side were the "nationally" minded, older members with a middle-class background who had originally founded the local party and opposing them was the party activist Kurt Daluege, a qualified engineer who had control of about 600 supporters. These men were almost without exception former soldiers from the front and fighters from the notorious right extremist Freikorps, who had been deeply disappointed by Germany's defeat in World War I. By 1924 they had already started violent attacks on liberal, left-wing and allegedly "Jewish-looking" Berliners, mainly in the elegant districts near the Kaiser Wilhelm Memorial Church. In 1926, Daluege, who had joined the Hitler movement back in 1923, took his men with him into the Berlin SA, the NSDAP band of thugs organised on paramilitary lines. Then in the summer he challenged the middle-class party members with this power base behind him. This struggle culminated in a mass punch-up between the supporters of both wings of the party in a public house called "Haverlands Festsäle" near the Hackescher Markt S-Bahn station.

Hitler had been watching the events in Berlin from Munich without taking any action, but now he got involved; he despatched his best young agitator, 29 year old Joseph Goebbels, to the capital as "Gauleiter" (District Party Chairman) . Goebbels arrived in Berlin on 9th November 1926, exactly three years after the "Führer's" failed Putsch in Munich. In the 19 years that followed, Goebbels controlled the Berlin NSDAP and his ruthlessness in the battle for Berlin made him one of Germany's major politicians. His diary entry on the evening of 8th November had read: "Into the fray!" and it was not long before the Gauleiter put words into action. His first clever tactical move was to make Daluege his deputy and thereby have the Berlin SA on his side; and he knew exactly what he wanted of them – brutality and effective publicity. After only five days in Berlin, Goebbels had 300 SA men march through the communist stronghold of Neukölln in order to provoke savage fighting. A series of similar operations followed, attracting wide-spread attention to the NSDAP which until now had been hardly mentioned or simply referred to as some sort of curiosity in the Berlin press. The first large brawls with the KPD (German Communist Party) in the boroughs of Spandau and "red" Wedding resulted in dozens of casualties on both sides, some of them with severe injuries.

This didn't worry Goebbels. On the contrary, he was pleased and continued with his tactics. On 20th March 1927 the violent punch ups escalated further: In a train from Trebbin (Brandenburg) to Berlin there was serious fighting between two dozen men of the Communist "Rotfront-kämpfer-Bund" and the numerically stronger SA, who happened to be sitting in the next carriage. Reinhold Muchow, a low-ranking NS official in Berlin described in a private report how the situation developed: "It was obvious to the SA they had to respond to this provocation. (...) At each station we unleashed a stone bombardment on the communist carriage. (...) Then we reached Lichterfeld-Ost station. The SA had to alight here. This was the climax." Here Hitler's men pulled the emergency brake and stormed the compartments of the communists, all of whom sustained serious injuries. Then the revved-up "brown-shirts" marched from the Lichterfeld S-Bahn station to Wittenbergplatz to listen to a speech by their Gauleiter, beating up any supposed "Jewish" Berliners and other opponents on the way. Goebbels complained in his diary the next evening that: "People blamed us." The Berliner Morgenpost, at that time the largest newspaper in Germany, demanded: "The streets should belong to peaceful citizens, not some demonstrators or other." The right-wing liberal Vossische Zeitung was more specific: "The National Socialists started things." A few weeks later the violence led to a ban on the NSDAP, but only inside Berlin itself. In the Weimar Republic, a state under the rule of law, it had not been understood that Hitler, Goebbels and the National Socialist Party would use any means they could to achieve power.

At the beginning this goal was a long way off. Exactly how far can be seen by looking at the NSDAP election results in Berlin; in the Reichstag election in 1928, when the Party was allowed to take part again, they gained just 1.6% of the vote which was significantly less than their aver-

The head of Berlin's SA, Walter Stennes (standing left) and Gauleiter Joseph Goebbels compete for the leadership of the Nazi supporters in the capital. Photo probably originates from April 1928.

age in the rest of the country (2.6%). In the next few years, however, their progress was meteoric. Between 1928 and Hitler's appointment as Reich Chancellor in 1933, there were a total of 12 elections in Berlin; no fewer than three Reichstag elections, three for the Prussian State Landtag (State Parliament), two local elections and two ballots for the office of German Reich President. With each election the NSDAP share of the vote rose steadily – from the meagre 1.6% in 1928 to a massive 24.6% in the summer of 1932. Compared with the results across the whole nation those in the Reichstag constituency of Berlin (the only one in Germany whose borders were the same as those of the city itself) were always at the lower end, higher only than those in the strongly catholic constituency of Köln-Aachen. It has often been maintained that Berlin was one of the regions where the National Socialists were least popular, but this is a misleading statement. When the Berlin results are not compared with the numbers in other constituencies (including its own outlying rural areas where the NSDAP support was much stronger) but only with those in other big cities, it is clear that when ranked with the 15 largest cities in Germany, Berlin comes about halfway, as does Munich. In Bremen, Stuttgart, Dortmund, Essen and Duisburg, for example, the NSDAP found less support.

The National Socialist stronghold in the capital was the solidly middle-class borough of Steglitz and similarly well-to-do districts like Schöneberg, Wilmersdorf and Charlottenburg turned out in greater numbers for

In 1932 Adolf Hitler runs for election as Reich President against the current Reich President Paul von Hindenburg. Passers-by in Kreuzberg study the new NSDAP election posters.

the NSDAP. In the working class boroughs of Wedding, Prenzlauer Berg and Friedrichshain, Hitler's Party attracted significantly fewer votes. In the total results for Berlin the other boroughs were either just over or just under the average. At the beginning it was mainly white collar workers and the middle-class who voted for Hitler's Party, both in Berlin and throughout Germany; those people who were particularly frightened of social decline, with male voters slightly in the majority.
Between 1930 and 1932 the NSDAP gradually became a "Peoples' Protest Party", capable of winning votes in all strata of society, even among workers and the unemployed.

It was essentially Joseph Goebbels who was responsible for this. Despite several bans on the Party or SA for excesses of violence, he succeeded in selling the NSDAP to the middle-classes as a means to combat the threat of communism and the universally feared "Bolshevik Revolution". In the process the Gauleiter was just as ruthless with his own people as he was with his enemies and he overcame three Putsch attempts within the Berlin SA. Under their new leader, Walther Stennes, this troop of thugs had enlisted numerous members, but

An SA "Guard of Honour" at Horst Wessel's grave on the day after his burial in the St.Nikolai cemetery in Prenzlauer Berg.

they attached much more importance to the "socialist" messages of the NSDAP manifesto than the Party leadership. Goebbels, by contrast, wanted an outward demonstration of the rise of the NSDAP and by working for a just a few weeks in the "Opium Den" in Potsdamer Strasse, he raised sufficient funds from wealthy NS followers to move into "suitably appropriate" offices in Lützowstrasse in the borough of Tiergarten. The conflict escalated; in 1928 Stennes and many of his allies publicly resigned from Hitler's Party and only allowed themselves to be persuaded to return because of generous concessions. In 1930, Stennes and his loyal SA men stormed the Gauleiter's offices and it was Hitler's personal visit which prevented a split in the Party just before the important elections. Finally, in 1931, when Stennes was supposed to be replaced, he occupied Goebbels' offices again and for two days he took over Goebbels' newspaper, "Der Angriff". At this point the "Führer" expelled the rebellious Berlin SA leader and the Gauleiter managed to regain control of the NS followers.

As the Party membership grew Goebbels now started to increase the size of the headquarters of the "Berlin Gau" at reg-

Anti-Nazi demonstration on 1st May 1932 in the Lustgarten. Three arrows have been sewn on to the captured swastika flag – the symbol of the Social Democrat "Iron Front".

ular intervals, on average every 18 months. First it was moved further west to Willhelmplatz in Charlottenburg (today Richard-Wagner-Platz) then back towards the city centre in Hedemannstrasse, Kreuzberg and finally, in October 1932, to 11, Vossstrasse, more or less at the back of the Government Headquarters. All these "Gau" offices of the Berlin NSDAP were destroyed in the allied bombing or were demolished when the city was rebuilt.

The rise, the problems and the fall of the Berlin NSDAP can be followed in minute detail in Goebbels' diary, which he kept on an almost daily basis. It has to be said, however, that these diary entries were never subjectively honest reflections but were from a propagandist perspective right from the beginning. Goebbels had always planned to publish his notes as books and the first one, with the significant title, "The Battle for Berlin. The Beginning 1926/27", appeared in 1932. Nearly every violent act was turned round to sound like a "signal". When his SA troops stormed the premiere of the anti-war film, "All Quiet on the Western Front", about Erich Maria Remarque's novel of the same name and the performance license required in those days was subsequently withdrawn, Goebbels called it a victory for "Nationalist German". Every SA death was depicted as martyrdom – whether it was like Hans-Georg Kütemeyer, who fell into the Landwehr canal in 1928 in a drunken stupor or like the charismatic SA leader, Horst Wessel, who was shot during an argument with his landlady. Goebbels even wanted to stylize Wessel's funeral into a Party "Triumphal Procession", but the police put a stop to this on the grounds that only ten vehicles for the deceased's friends and relatives could be permitted. So instead, Goebbels staged an act of provocation - an SA march past the Communist Headquarters on Bülowplatz (today Rosa-Luxemburg-Platz). The "brown-shirts" were behaving with such brutality that in 1930 Prussia issued a general ban on uniform whereupon Goebbels told his followers to all appear in white shirts.

At this stage, however, there is no way that the NSDAP had "secured" power in and over Germany and least of all on the streets of Berlin. Until January 1933 it wasn't the rise of National Socialism, but rather of Social Democracy and above all Communism which was dominating the city

After the ban on uniforms for the SA in 1930, Goebbels has all his henchmen appear in white shirts.

landscape, although since 1929 there had not been a majority for the Democrats in Berlin. In the local elections the three explicitly anti-constitutional parties of the Weimar Republic, the KPD, the NSDAP and the German National Party (DNVP) (which had veered strongly to the right under their new leader, the press baron Alfred Hugenberg), had gained 48% of the votes – almost as many as the SPD, the Liberal splinter parties and the Catholic Centre put together (48.7%). In the subsequent Reichstag election in September 1930 their share had increased to 57.7%; democracy had collapsed in the German capital long before Adolf Hitler became Reich Chancellor.

Brutal Triumph

Transfer of power

In the New Year of 1932/33 the NSDAP appeared to have passed its peak, not only in Berlin but all over Germany as well. Their election results had been sinking since 1932. Important Nazi officials were rejecting Hitler's strategy of "all or nothing" (the Reich Chancellorship or total opposition) and were ready to allow the NSDAP to be a junior partner in a "National cabinet" and the Party was living well beyond its financial means.

In the German capital there was an increasing feeling of relief. In its 1933 New Year edition for example, the liberal Berliner Tagesblatt, the most respected newspaper in Germany, mocked Hitler: "All over the world people were talking about - what was his first name - Adalbert Hitler. Some time in the future? Missing, presumed dead!" In assessing the stranglehold that the National Socialists and the Communists had exerted on the State in the past year, the editor of the Vossische Zeitung happily concluded that, "In spite of this, the Republic has been saved – not because it has been defended, but because its attackers have finished each other off."

In fact, Hitler had done little to achieve his aim. In 1932 he had taken part in two exploratory discussions with Reich President Paul von Hindenburg but had twice antagonised the aged but extremely status conscious Field Marshal with his demands. Hindenburg might have appointed the NSDAP "Führer" as "perhaps - Postmaster General" in a coalition government, but not as Reich Chancellor even if his party had formed the strongest faction by a good margin. On top of this, Hitler had internal party problems; his extravagant life-style set the brown-shirts, of whom by now there were several thousands – against him. In Munich Hitler lived in a luxurious nine room apartment and used as an office a whole floor of the "Brown House", a city mansion near Königsplatz, which had been turned into the Party Headquarters. Since 1931 he had been staying regularly in the most expensive hotel in the capital, the "Kaiserhof" on Wilhelmsplatz opposite the Reich Chancellery. Today, the North Korean Embassy stands on the site of this exclusive hotel on the former Wilhelmsplatz (Mohrenstrasse underground station). Of course, Hitler was using the hotel accommodation as a political statement; the NSDAP leader was announcing his claim to a top

A column of SA man in a deliberately provocative procession past the Communist Headquarters on Bülow Platz (now Rosa-Luxemburg-Platz).

position in a future government. He never stayed there alone but always had an entourage of about a dozen people which sometimes took up half a floor of the "Kaiserhof". Hitler practically held court here, received visitors and kept petitioners waiting. In the winter of 1931/32, at the height of the economic crisis, many of Hitler's followers were out of work and his extravagance, partly financed by their membership subscriptions, must have struck them as presumptuous and provoking. In fact in the last weeks of 1932 an unusually high number of SA men went over to the Communists and surprisingly the front between the left-wing and right-wing extremists had generally weakened. At the beginning of November the KPD and the NSDAP had staged a joint strike at the Berlin Transport Company (BVG), against the wishes of the unions and the SPD. After five days and several deaths the industrial action crumbled and Goebbels noted a very "muted atmosphere" in the Berlin NSDAP, which was doubtless expressing things mildly. In December the Party faced division; a dramatic appearance by Hitler in front of NS officials in the "Kaiserhof", at which the Party leader is even supposed to have threatened suicide, prevented the split.

Despite being pretty shattered, even at the beginning of 1933 the "Führer" still continued to exert considerable influence over millions of followers and the former Reich Chancellor, Franz von Papen, wanted to exploit this situation. In 1932 von Papen had led the government for six months as the front man of the strongly conservative circles around the Minister for the Army, Kurt von Schleicher. This supposed puppet, a not very gifted but extremely ambitious schemer, had enjoyed his position as Reich Chancellor and wanted to get back into power after his removal from office in November 1932. At the beginning of January Papen began to play a game of high stakes; he promised Hitler the post of Reich Chancellor in charge of a reactionary cabinet in which he would appoint himself as Deputy Reich Chancellor. What he didn't tell the "Führer" was that those who shared his views, mainly members of the anti-democratic DNVP, were intending to "frame" Hitler and his two NSDAP Ministers in the cabinet. In this way Papen was expecting to be able to "enlist" the masses of the Hitler movement for his own reactionary policies. He stalled all criticism of his plan by his allies: "What do you want then! I have Hindenburg's trust. In two months we have forced Hitler into a corner so that he's squealing." At the same time the similarly hard line conservative, but anti-Papen Army Chiefs were vehemently against Hitler's appointment as Reich Chancellor. On 26th January 1933, when Papen was almost watching the closing stages of his game of intrigue, General Kurt von Hammerstein-Equord warned the Reich President of the dangers of trusting the leader of the NSDAP with the business of government. Hindenburg is said to have responded with the words: "Gentlemen, surely you don't think that I am capable of appointing that Austrian Corporal to Reich Chancellor of Germany."

The weekend of 28th/29th January 1933 changed everything. A sensational rumour went round Berlin; the German Army intended to stage a putsch to stop Hitler's appointment as Reich Chancellor. The Potsdam garrison would march into the government district and keep the Reich President under house arrest. Reich Chancellor Kurt von Schleicher, who had just officially resigned, would dissolve the Reichstag and rule as dictator for one or two years. On the Sunday Papen informed Hindenburg of the rumour and Hitler and Goebbels heard about it in the Gauleiter's elegant apartment on Reichskanzlerplatz (today Theodor-Heuss-Platz) in Chlarlottenburg. As a "counter-measure" they ordered the mobilisation of the SA and waited until five o'clock in the morning for the alleged coup d'état. But nothing happened – apart from the fact that on this Sunday Hindenburg gave in to pressure from Papen and accepted the cabinet he had assembled, with Hitler at its helm. Schleicher, Hammerstein and the German Army had never intended to stage a putsch; the rumour had simply started through a series of misunderstandings and the ill-fated work of a self-appointed "intermediary" in a highly political Berlin. Nevertheless, on the following morning, 30th January 1933, against his better judgement the Reich President appointed the "Führer" of the NSDAP as leader of the government – not, incidentally, according to protocol at 73, Wilhelmstrasse, in the Reich Presidential residence, which was being renovated at the time, but in the Reich Chancellor's residence at 77, Wilhelmstrasse, where Hindenburg was living

SA block off the Hotel "Kaiserhof" where Hitler is staying. (30th January 1933)

The "Führer" of the NSDAP makes an appearance on the hotel balcony for his supporters (propaganda shot).

during the renovations. On this site today, where on the final night of the Weimar Republic Hindenburg had awaited a military revolution, stand the last prefabricated buildings so typical of those erected in the GDR era.

Hitler's appointment was by no means welcomed by all Berliners. In the Berliner Morgenpost on 31st January 1933 their readers were told to be "vigilant and distrusting" and the newspaper promised: "From now on we shall have to examine the actions of the new government to check whether they are in accordance with the constitution to which they have sworn an oath. We shall remain completely calm and objective. We shall not allow ourselves to be provoked and recommend that everyone who finds this change of government unedifying does the same." On the other hand the liberal journalists of the Ullstein press were not expecting that Hitler would not be interested in the usual traditions of democratic politics. In any case the Politbüro of the KPD (The "Politbüro" was the name given to the Communist Party executive committee) did not stick to the recommendation of not giving a pretext for starting a fight. On the contrary, Ernst Thälmann's aides invited their followers to launch attacks on the NSDAP and the police. During the very first night of Hitler's government the communists shot dead an SA leader and a policeman in a brawl in Charlottenburg. This double shooting was a godsend for the new government; they could now start to quell the apparently immediate threat of a "bolshevic revolution" with brutal violence. In July 1932 Franz von Papen had ruthlessly brought the largely social democratic Prussian police force and administration in line with his reactionary policies and so the new Minister for the Interior, Herman Göring, was able to deploy a compliant instrument against the KPD and the SPD. After the new cabinet had only been in office for 72 hours, it became immediately clear that Hitler would not be satisfied with the extent of his powers; he would not allow himself to be "framed" nor "commit himself" and certainly not be "pushed into the background". With equal speed the

Passers-by look at the burnt-out Reichstag from in front of the Brandenburg Gate.

The gutted debating chamber of the parliament building.

Army Generals learned of Hitler's plans. On 3rd February 1933, in the same rooms of the Bendlerblock in Tiergartenstrasse where eleven and a half years later, on 20th July 1944, Graf Stauffenberg's plot would fail, the new Reich Chancellor informed the military Chiefs of Staff of the "expansion of the "Lebensraum" of the German people, if necessary with weapons." In other words - war.

Total power by conquest

To achieve this aim, however, the "Führer" had to gain complete control over Germany. As early as February 1933 he began his first war – against his enemies at home and the German capital was the most important, if not the only battlefield. The extremely easy transfer of governmental control to Hitler was followed by the brutal conquest of total power by the NSDAP. The KPD and SPD newspapers and even those run by other political parties were immediately banned on grounds of triviality and the SA roamed the streets of Berlin with increasing violence, hunting down any "communist revolutionaries". On 17th February Goering issued the order: "Police officers who use their guns in the course of their duties will have my full protection, regardless of the consequences of their actions." Put simply: shoot first and ask later. Five days later 50,000 SA and SS men were appointed as "Auxiliary Policeman". The authors of the violence on the streets thus became the instruments of state power. Under these conditions a fair campaign for the new Reichstag elections, which Hitler had immediately called, was out of the question. This was of course intentional; the new Reich Chancellor wanted to turn the vote into a triumphant plebiscite in order to gain total power.

An almost incredible coincidence then came to his aid. On the evening of 21st February, Marinus van der Lubbe, a Dutch anarchist got into the Reichstag and set it on fire using such primitive materials as fire lighters and torches made out of tablecloths.

Berlin Police search and occupy the KPD (German Communist Party) Central Office on Bülowplatz on 2nd February 1933.

The fire was enormous and reduced the whole parliamentary chamber to ashes. Two days previously, van der Lubbe, a mentally confused invalid, had already started fires at four other places in Berlin, but they had all been discovered in time. The Reichstag fire was the lunatic's first success and by the time the fire brigade reached the parliament building the fire was out of control and the flames could no longer be extinguished. There has been speculation ever since that Lubbe was only a front man and that in fact a troop of SA men had set the parliament on fire. However, all the "evidence" that has been used for this argument has proved to consist of misinterpretations, rumours or bad forgeries. Hitler, Goebbels and Goering were actually completely surprised by van der Lubbe's arson, but they immediately made use of it for own purposes. In the same night arrests were made all over Prussia and above all in Berlin, using lists that had been drawn up by the political police as early as the Autumn of 1932 – before Hitler was Reich Chancellor.

The lucky ones among the social democrats, left-wing intellectuals and other Hitler opponents were arrested by the police and taken to the normal detention centres; the unlucky ones fell into the hands of the "Auxiliary Police" of the SA or SS and were locked up in one of several dozen hastily improvised prisons. One of these was the equipment shed of the water tower in Prenzlauer Berg and also numerous SA "assault centres", mostly the back rooms or store rooms of ordinary pubs. In these practically lawless rooms the SA mercilessly beat up and tortured their victims; more than 20 people were murdered in Berlin during the

SS guarding abducted Hitler opponents in one of the many improvised torture cellars.

seven days following the Reichstag fire. It is impossible to say exactly how many of these torture chambers (later called "unofficial KZs") existed in the capital in the early days of March but several thousand NS opponents were interrogated there in the days leading up to the Reichstag elections on 5th March. The state only intervened if the SA suddenly became really savage. On 3rd March 1933, for example, at 20, Wilhelmstrasse, Spandau, the police prevented several prisoners being executed and on 29th March, when a police riot squad even stormed the Berlin SA Headqarters in Hedemannstrasse, Kreuzberg, and freed the men held there. The brown-shirts had made these arrests in the Berlin stock exchange and Göring could not countenance the seizure of such financially influential men. But such events were exceptions. As a rule the Nazi "Auxiliary Police" abducted, arrested and tortured whoever they wanted, completely unhindered and in this way of course many old accounts were settled. Since 28th February 1933 there had even existed a formal legal basis for these violent excesses. Hindenburg's "Reichstag fire decree" declared first a "civil state of emergency" in accordance with the relevant paragraphs in the Weimar Constitution, then suspended most basic and civil rights and heavily increased the punishment for alleged or actual political crimes. The reaction in Berlin to the explosion of violence in March and April 1933 was palpable. Members of the communist factions were severely ill-treated by the SA hordes and many of them disappeared underground. Scores of SPD officials also fell into the hands of the torturers. Yet the lower and middle classes did not revolt against this patently NSDAP brutality and nor did the military or the organised working classes. This was because support for the National Socialists had now become widespread. On 12th March 1933 in the (last) local elections, 984,467 Berliners voted for Hitler which represented 40% of the 2.5 million votes cast overall and about as many as the KPD and SPD had polled jointly.

At the beginning of March 1933 Hitler and the NSDAP more or less controlled the German capital and the cabinet was already essentially powerless. However the reactionaries around Papen and Hugenberg not only didn't notice that Hitler would not be "pushed into the background", they obediently fell into insignificance. Now the NSDAP began to extend their power into the other parts of Germany, mainly using the same methods as they had in Berlin. Thousands of actual or alleged opponents of Nazism were taken away and tortured. Dozens of them were murdered. The largest wave of emigration in Germany history began. It was above all KPD officials, intellectuals and wealthy citizens from a Jewish background who realised that they were no longer safe in their homeland. On 23rd March 1933 the NSDAP made a temporary halt to extending their power. On this day Hitler assembled the newly elected representative body of the people in the Kroll Opera House, a building opposite the burnt out Reichstag, which was empty at the time (now this site to the south of the Federal Republic Chancellor's office is a stretch of lawn) and passed a sweeping "Enabling Act". The KPD representatives had already been stripped of their mandates and of the remaining parliamentary parties; only the Social Democrats had the courage to vote against Hitler. Otto Wels, the leader of the SPD at the time, made a speech which enraged the Reich Chancellor but the bill got the necessary majority to effect a constitutional amendment. The Enabling Act, which conferred all power on the Reich Chancellor, remained the legal basis of Adolf Hitler's rule force until the suicide of the "Führer and Reich Chancellor" on 30th April 1945. It formed the Basic Law of the Third Reich.

Armed with this new authority Hitler now set about stabilising his power base. Within a few months public life in Germany had been completely turned upside down by a raft of laws. By the summer the government had banned all other political parties, if they hadn't already dissolved themselves. More than 10,000 Nazi opponents were held in the "unofficial KZs" of the SA and the first official concentration camps like Dachau near Munich and

On 1st August 1933 SPD politicians are taken away to the Oranienburg concentration camp just outside Berlin.

Oranienburg just outside Berlin. In the capital itself the barracks on General-Pape-Strasse (partially still standing) and the military detention centre on Columbiadamm (today the site of north-east wing of the Tempelhof Airport building and a scarcely noticed memorial to the inmates of the Columbia-Haus KZ) were used as prisons and torture chambers. The end of June 1933 witnessed a particularly appalling excess of violence during the first months of Nazi rule. In Köpenick, a south-east borough of Berlin, SA troops gruesomely murdered at least 25 people, mainly trade union officials, communists and social democrats, in the space of five days. This wave of murders has gone down in history as the "Köpenick week of blood" and at the main scene of the crime, the district court on Puchanstrasse, there is today a memorial to the victims.

Popular Dictatorship

"Falling into line"

Despite the unprecedented wave of violence during the first six months of 1933 there was widespread approval for Hitler and his politics. In the Reichstag elections on 5th March 1933, 17.4 million Germans (43.9%) had voted for Hitler, among them 400,000 Berliners (31.3%). Whilst this was not a majority, it was an enormous number. On any given occasion Goebbels and his Berlin NSDAP had no problems in mobilising tens of thousands of enthusiastic followers, even if this number was not as high as the Gauleiter, now promoted to Minister for Propaganda, liked to claim in his diary and in the newspapers. In the first few months of Hitler's government the NSDAP attracted new members on a massive scale, mainly for reasons of opportunism. In the end, after membership had tripled, the party called a halt to new subscriptions on 1st May 1933. It is not known exactly how many of the capital's population became "party comrades" during these weeks, but it is certain to have been a very large number. A derisive nickname for those new recruits who eagerly offered their services to the new dictators soon crept into the Berlin vernacular – they were referred to as, "March Heroes", alluding cynically to the description of the rebels who fell at the barricades in March 1848. At the same time a process of "falling in line" began in large sections of Berlin society and indeed all over Germany. At the venerable Friedrich-Wilhelms-Universität on Unter den Linden (now Humboldt-Universität) the members of the National Socialist Student Union expelled staff who were either Jewish or known to be left-wing; almost 250 lecturers were forced to leave the University. The political climate there had already been revealed in the elections to the student council the previous year, when two thirds of the Berlin students voted for the NSDAP.

Even more shameful was the behaviour of many Berlin journalists. In January 1933, alongside the conservative Scherl-Verlag controlled by the leader of the DNVP, Alfred Hugenberg, and the National Socialist publications such as the Völkischer Beobachter and the Angriff, there were two big publishers: the Moses-Verlag, whose publications included the most influential German newspaper, the Berliner Tagesblatt, and the Ullstein-Verlag, Europe's largest newspaper publisher's, which owned the Berliner Morgenpost, the newspaper with the largest circulation in the country, the

Berliners sitting round the base of the Victory Column (which was then on the square in front of the Reichstag) listening to the transmission of one of Hitler's speeches in May 1935.

Vossische Zeitung, an important voice of the bourgeoisie and the B.Z. am Mittag, in its time the "fastest" paper of the press in the world. Both publishers were run by liberal German-Jewish families. After Hitler's appointment as Reich Chancellor it became clear that in both companies there were journalists who to some extent shared the National Socialists' views and who also caught wind of a good career move. In nearly all the editorial offices the pressure to adapt to the wishes of the new government built up. The NS sympathisers soon exerted great influence over the formation of public opinion. With the help of an anonymous corporate finance company "Cautio Ltd", it was easy enough for the NSDAP to swallow up the Mosse-Verlag because it had been insolvent since the autumn of 1932. The strong man of the NS press (and Goebbels' competitor), Max Amann, needed slightly longer to take over the Ullstein-Press, but in 1934 he had control here too. The Ullstein brothers were forced to sell their company to "Cautio" at a price far below its value and before this all Jewish journalists had already been dismissed. Even radio, still a new medium at this time and under the direct control of the State, quickly became totally dependent. On the evening of 30th January 1933 the "Reichsfunk" radio stations in Stuttgart and Munich had succeeded in refusing to broadcast Goebbels' first address, but a week later the NS Minister for Home Affairs, Wilhelm Frick, had gained total control over the radio journalists. Here too young careerists were promoted to replace colleagues who had either been removed or remained critical of the regime. The way that Berlin journalism, once so self-confident, fell in line with the Nazis is the greatest defeat that this profession has ever experienced.

In almost all walks of Berlin society the same thing happened as in the University and the press. The economy adapted to the new order, as did wide sections of the Protestant Church. In the Martin Luther Memorial Church in Marienfelde a bust of Hitler was even erected in the lobby and in the pulpit a uniformed Hitler Youth can still be seen on one of the reliefs. The workers stood by and watched as the unions were crushed. Hitler had made a clever tactical move in declaring 1st May 1933 the "National Workers' Holiday". On the morning of 2nd May SA troops occupied the union bases, disbanded their organisations and incorporated all workers in the newly created "German Workers' Front". This happened all over Germany as well as in Berlin, but it was in the capital where the changes usually first took effect. On 12th November 1933, in the first "election" of the Third Reich where only a "unified list of candidates" which voters could either approve or otherwise, 85.1% of Berliners voted for Hitler. Of course, the voting slips were all numbered so that a secret ballot no longer existed. The actual percentage of Berliners who agreed with Hitler was therefore certainly lower; but whether it was 60, 70 or 80% is naturally pure speculation.

The beginning of the persecution of the Jews

The German-Jewish population had been suffering from attacks by Hitler's followers since 1924. All through the years of the Weimar Republic shop windows were repeatedly smashed in and Nazi pamphlets stirred up hatred against "Jewish" Berlin department stores such as Wertheim and Tietz (Hertie). Even before 1933 Goebbels had on various occasions directed his SA men to specifically target Berlin Jews. But as violent as some of these attacks had been, they did not seem even worth mentioning in comparison with the brutal acts that were to follow after 30th January. On 17th February the Nazis stormed an examination at the Staatliche Kunsthochschule (State Art Academy) in Charlottenburg (today the University of the Arts on Hardenbergstrasse) and beat up the "Jewish" Professors. On the night of the Reichstag fire SA men attacked the Berlin offices of the Jewish "Central Club" and during the weeks that followed they abducted numerous Jews, mostly still because they were KPD or SPD officials, not because of their religion or their "Jewish race". The majority were tortured and some were killed. The first Berlin Jew who was murdered for his faith was probably Siegbert Kindermann, an 18 year old baker's apprentice. A year earlier he had gone to the police to report harassment by an SA man who on 18th March 1933 sought his gruesome revenge. Many more victims followed – nobody knows exactly how many and yet the Deputy Reich Chancellor, Franz von Papen, tried to calm things down by writing to the German-American Chamber of Commerce. As

SA men blockade the shops owned by Jews on 1st April 1933 – pictured is a clothes shop on the Kurfürstendamm.

the New York Times reported on 29th March, the man who had helped Hitler come to power stressed in his official letter that there had been "less than a dozen" attacks on Jews with US passports and that there were hundreds of thousands of German Jews who were living unmolested.

The new rulers, however, wanted to change all this. Since the Nazis had taken over, it was the lower ranks which were particularly keen to start hitting out at the "Jewry". Together with Goebbels, the Gauleiter of the NSDAP in Franken, Julius Streicher, an ardent antisemite and publisher of the propagandist paper "Der Stürmer", took the wishes of their party comrades to heart and got Hitler to declare that on Saturday, 1st April Jewish shops all over German would be boycotted. On the previous night NS followers stuck large posters on the advertising columns of the capital without any regard for the (paid-for) adverts already there. They bore the words: "Jews have until 10 o'clock on Saturday to think things over. Then the battle begins. Jews all over the world want to destroy Germany. German people! Defend yourselves! Don't buy your goods from Jews!" Part of the poster was written in two languages, in German and in English, because the pretext for the boycott was the fact that British and American newspapers were considering declaring an economic embargo against Germany and there had never been any concrete measures taken by international governments. The photos of SA men, standing in front of shop entrances, went round the world. Some of them were holding printed signs calling for a boycott and others had handwritten slogans like, "Danger! Jews get out!" or "Look out Itzig! Go to Palestine!". KaDeWe on Wittenbergplatz and other

"Jewish" department stores stayed shut, but Karstadt on Hermannplatz remained open; the day before the management had dismissed all Jewish employees "as a precaution".

Joseph Goebbels noted enthusiastically in his diary: "All along the Tauentzien. Everything under boycott. Exemplary discipline. An impressive spectacle. Everything going calmly." But in reality the "Jew boycott" was not a success in Berlin. It's true that in the main shopping areas – on the Kurfürstendamm, on Potsdamerplatz and Alexanderplatz as well as in Friedrichstrasse and Leipzigerstrasse – there were groups of people watching the SA guards and sometimes cheering them on; the Frankfurter Zeitung reported from the capital that the boycott ended up like a "Peoples' festival". However, the anti-Semitic spark did not ignite the majority of Berliners as Goebbels and Streicher were hoping. People were only afraid to enter the "Jewish shops" where SA troops were deployed; some Berliners met with no resistance when they consciously disregarded the boycott, for example the writer Erich Ebermayer: "There are two SA men standing in front of the entrance, but the shop is not closed. You can go inside and buy something if you have the courage. M. and I have the courage (...) When we step inside the shop the SA man says to us each time in a totally polite, disciplined manner: 'Jewish Shop!' Just as courteously and calmly we reply: 'Thank you, we know that.' An astonished look from the SA man, but never any rudeness." In Kronenstrasse, Mitte, where Berliners could buy exclusive clothes, trade was a lot worse than on normal Saturdays, but there were still customers despite the SA guards standing in front of many of the shops.

International reaction to the boycott was disastrous. For instance the British Ambassador reported back to his Foreign Minister: "In my opinion it would therefore be a mistake to condemn the whole German Nation for a measure which has not just aroused the outrage and abhorrence of the Diplomatic Corps but also of many Germans themselves." In view of the unsatisfactory support by Berliners and the negative effect abroad Goebbels did not extend the one day boycott. Together with all his accomplices he found other ways to oppress the 160,000 Jews in Berlin. On 1st April all Jewish doctors working for the State were dismissed; on 3rd April all Jewish teachers were "sent on leave"; on 7th April all the grants for kindergartens in the Jewish community were withdrawn and three days later the financial support for Jewish pupils in need was also stopped. In the same period Jewish children were banned from using the public swimming pool in Gartenstrasse (Mitte). Also on 7th April the "law for restoring the civil service with tenure" came into force all over Germany, requiring that all Jewish state employees would be dismissed. From this point onwards Jews were gradually banned from any activity that occurred to the resourceful civil servants. It certainly wasn't only or even especially the NS officials who had the perverse imagination to make the lives of the Jewish Berliners increasingly difficult. Those responsible were mainly local civil servants who wanted to show proof of their "reliability" when it came to carrying out Hitler's policies.

A nationwide action began, "Against the un-German spirit", which meant against Jews or any other supposed "foreign ele-

At the end of April 1933 the police use arbitrary "raids" to increase the pressure on Berlin Jews, here in Grenadier- and Dragonerstrasse in Mitte.

ments". All over the world this slogan came to symbolise the contempt in which the politics of Hitler's "New Germany" held humanity. On 10th May 1933 on Opernplatz (today Bebelplatz) directly opposite the Friedrich-Wilhelms-Universität, undesirable books publicly went up in flames. Among the authors whose works Berlin students threw on to a huge funeral pyre were the German Jews, Theodor Wolff and Emil Ludwig, but also atheists like Karl Marx and Karl Kautsky and also Sigmund Freud and Erich Maria Remarque, Kurt Tucholsky, Carl von Ossietzky and Erich Kästner. Kästner even had the dubious honour of witnessing the event. He recalled later: "In the year 1933 my books were burnt with sinister pomp and ceremony by a certain Mr Goebbels on a large square next to the State Opera House in Berlin. He triumphantly called out the names of twenty four German writers who were to be symbolically obliterated for ever. I was the only one of these twenty four who had personally appeared to attend this theatrical impudence. I stood in front of the University, hemmed in between students in SA uniform, the pride of our nation. I saw our books flying into the licking flames and heard the schmaltzy tirades of the cunning little liar. Funereal weather hung over the city." In Goebbels' diary the account is rather different: "Then late in the evening a speech on Opernplatz. In front of the funeral pyre of dirty and trashy literature burnt by the students. I am on top form."

In Berlin this piece of theatre certainly did not meet with any enthusiasm, but

On 10th May 1933 Berlin students burn the books of "unaccepted" and Jewish writers on Opernplatz (today Bebelplatz).

rather indifference. About 200,000 volumes were burnt on this evening and the writer Stefan Zweig wrote to a friend in Leipzig: "That ceremony which was organised with my books did not please me at all, because outside Germany I am now regarded as a hero and martyr – something I am certainly not. Incidentally, I would never have thought that this little incident would have attracted so much attention abroad." The Third Reich had shown its true face as Heinrich Heine already knew in 1822: "That was just the prelude; where books are burnt so will be people." Today, underneath Bebelplatz, a room full of empty book-shelves designed by the Israeli artist Micha Ullman is a permanent reminder of the burning of the books.

Hitler and the capital

Soon after he was appointed Reich Chancellor, Hitler took up permanent residence in the service flat of the Reich Chancellery in Wilhelmstrasse. He didn't have to move very far because since 1931, whenever he was in the capital he stayed in the "Kaiserhof" on Wilhelmsplatz. The NSDAP leader never owned a private apartment in Berlin, neither before nor after 1933. His official home remained Munich. When the "Führer" spent time there he regularly sought out his old haunts, something he never did in Berlin. He only left the Reich Chancellery for official appointments or to pay his most important followers a private visit in their own homes. For example he was regularly a guest of the Goebbels family on the Havel island of Schwanenwerder. In 1939 the Reich Chancellery bought "as stock" an impressive house near the Propaganda Minister's villa, but Hitler never seems to have set foot in this "Aryanised" building which had been extorted from its Jewish owner at a price far below its value. There are no records to prove whether the "Führer" ever visited his half-brother, Alois Hitler who lived at 2, Wittenbergplatz. He also only went to museums, the theatre or opera in an official capacity; several of the latter had had "a 'Führer' box" built in the Dress Circle, directly opposite the stage. When the Admiralspalast in Friedrichstrasse underwent alterations in 1939, the architect responsible, Paul Baumgarten, unfortunately forgot to include one which caused considerable problems. In 1941 a separate box had to be "added as a modernisation" so that Hitler would still attend performances. This box still exists and "adorns" the auditorium of the since re-named Metropol Theatre.

State occasion on "Heroes' Remembrance Day" in the Berlin State Opera House on 8th March 1936. (Adolf Hitler standing in the "Führer's Box" above the swastika flag.)

Hitler's complete lack of interest in Berlin life has given rise to the view that the "Führer" rejected the German capital and after 1945 this is the way Berlin writers, in particular, boosted morale. However, this comforting idea does not stand up to closer inspection. Over the twelve year period of his rule Hitler was in his allegedly unloved capital more often than anywhere else, in fact on average he was there for one day in three whereas he only stayed at his "Berghof", above Berchtesgaden one day in four. Up to and including1940 he clearly spent the majority of days each year in Berlin, although in 1938 he spent only slightly longer in the Reich Chancellery than in the Alps.

This statistical evidence is matched by the fact that Hitler spoke very positively about Berlin, both in his speeches and privately. At the celebration held to mark the building of the Reich Chancellery (Richtfest), he said "Therefore it is my aim to give this new and greater Empire a worthy capital (...) In its grandeur the capital is to express the greatness of the State." But he also made many negative comments (often made at almost the same time as the positive ones). These statements by Hitler contained remarks criticising Berlin, often sharply and scornfully. It is exactly this kind of ambivalence that is so typical of Hitler whose thinking, apart from his two basic tenets – racial mania and the battle for "living space"

Berlin celebrates the "Anschluss" with Austria. Thousands cheer Hitler (standing in the open car) on 16th March 1938 on the Belle-Alliance-Strasse (today Mehringdamm).

– was eclectic and changed with the wind to the point of being quite arbitrary.

During the war the inconsistency of his statements about Berlin did not alter. For example in July 1941 he told his guests that it would be "no loss" if Berlin were destroyed by bombs. Three months later he announced to the almost identical group around the table: "I've always liked Berlin and if it worries me that there's a lot which is not so nice there, then it's only because the city means something to me." Admittedly in 1941 the "Führer" spent much less time in the capital – precisely 57 days; in the following year it was 25 days and in 1943 just 10 days. Yet in 1945 Hitler decided against going to Berchtesgaden, where he could have withdrawn to a large, totally secure and comfortably furnished system of mountain galleries, but to the much smaller, unfinished and more dangerous "Führerbunker". One can only speculate about the reasons; the most probable is that Hitler's ambivalent relationship with his capital included intense feelings of love-hate. It was in Berlin that he wanted to await the end.

The Berliners and the "Führer"

In the autumn of 1933 the NSDAP had more or less subjugated the entire capital. Before Hitler was appointed Reich Chancellor it had not been an easy ride; in free elections no more than a third of the electorate had vote for him. In the years to follow there are naturally no longer any serious statistics available – one can only use circumstantial evidence to get some idea of

Hitler appears at the window of the Reich Chancellery for his enthusiastic supporters (Photo from summer 1934).

the attitude of the Berliners. The section of the working class which had previously been staunchly communist remained largely hostile to Hitler. On the other hand, the majority of the more numerous skilled workers, who had mostly voted SPD during the Weimar Republic, soon accepted the new political circumstances. The Protestant middle class and the military were mostly pro-Hitler, although there were exceptions, for example Pastor Martin Niemöller's Confessional Church in the St. Annen parish of Dahlem. In the "better circles" of Berlin society there was, however, widespread hatred of the proletariat masses of the SA, but this "problem" was considered "resolved" when the SA Chief of Staff, Ernst Röhm and his close friends, was brutally eliminated in June 1934. Under Röhm the SA had demanded a "second revolution" to follow the "national revolution" of spring 1933; it was to be a "socialist revolution" in which German society would be re-structured. However, this was precisely what Hitler didn't want because in order to achieve his plans of conquest he needed the conservative officer corps of the German Army as the core of his invasion army. So he gave way to the game of intrigue being played by the SS, Gestapo and Army Chiefs and staged the alleged "Röhm-Putsch", in which along with SA leaders some declared opponents of the Nazis were murdered, including the former Reich Chancellor, Kurt Schleicher and his wife. Over the first weekend of July 1934, a total of 24 people in and around Berlin were shot dead by murder squads and Hitler dared to justify these murders as "state self-defence".

For the next few years until the beginning of the war, the NSDAP and Gauleiter Goebbels were no longer required to give "extra help" whenever enough Berliners were needed to provide an impressive turnout. This is backed up by foreign diplomats and correspondents, the official weekly film reports (although these could have been manipulated) and also private footage taken by amateur filmmakers. When Hitler was in the capital, thousands of Berliners would frequently assemble on Wilhelmsplatz, Mitte, hoping that the "Führer" would appear at the window of the Reich Chancellery or – from 1935 onwards – on the balcony specially built for this purpose. On the new National Socialist "public holidays" such as 30th January, the "Heroes' Day" in March, the "Führer's Birthday" on 20th April, the "Day of Work" on 1st May as well as 9th November in memory of the 1923 Putsch, there was always not only a huge number of flags "decorating" the government district and all public buildings, but also sufficient Berliners to cheer the various parades enthusiastically. For the Olympic Games in 1936, the State Visit of the Italian "Duce", Benito Mussolini in 1937 and Hitler's 50th birthday in 1939 there was on each occasion a crowd of over two million people lining the route. Even Goebbels couldn't have "staged" such enthusiasm – it came from the heart.

Yet the spies from the State Police Headquarters noted carefully any swings in public opinion and in March 1936, for example, they reported: "Behind closed doors there is dissatisfaction everywhere. It is indicative that only very few people now use the German greeting of 'Heil Hitler'. One can spend several days in the city without hearing it used at all, except by government officials and people in uniform

SA men standing on the corner of Wilhelmstrasse and Leipzigerstrasse in September 1937, waiting to be deployed as marshals.

or from the provinces." This is certainly an exaggerated description and moreover the real reason for the reluctance was not the NS leadership itself but its inevitable excesses. "People say that the effects of many of his subordinates' inadequacies cannot escape the Führer's attention; he must be aware how many of them are building themselves luxurious homes and how some of his colleagues are really provoking the population with their extravagant life-style."

Of course, not all Berliners had become convinced Nazis and only very few of them had read Hitler's indigestible book, "Mein Kampf". Pressure from the Gestapo also meant that no-one was inclined to voice their criticism. At the same time there were some very well organised campaigns directed against the total takeover by Nazi ideology. In December 1935 the workers of an AEG factory in Wedding fought a successful battle against having a "voluntary" contribution deducted from their wages (which had in any case been frozen) for the "winter relief organisation". The SPD in exile made a similar declaration from a Siemens factory in Lichtenberg and from an anonymous (for security reasons) building site in North Berlin. The newspapers did not run reports about such events and apart from hearsay, there were practically no other alternative ways of disseminating information. Up to 1939 no-one landed up in a concentration camp just for telling a joke or spreading a rumour, but anyone who distributed leaflets, exchanged information with Hitler's adversaries abroad or took part in meetings with opposition factions might find themselves in the torture chambers which since summer 1933 had been taken over by the

In December 1937 Japanese Officers visit Sachsenhausen concentration camp to the north of Berlin. In the background is the entrance to the prisoner area, "Tower A".

SS. In 1935 there were about 3,500 KZ (concentration camp) prisoners and "Reichsführer SS", Heinrich Himmler, who had become enormously influential since the "Röhm-Putsch" began to organise the camps down to the last detail. Inner-city camps were gradually being replaced by newly erected detention centres on the edge of large towns. For Berlin the Sachsenhausen KZ in Oranienburg took over from Columbia-Haus. At the end of 1936, six months after Sachsenhausen had opened, there were 1,300 detainees imprisoned there in a total area of 31 hectares. On 20th April 1945, the last "daily report" of the Camp Commandant at the main camp of Sachsenhausen listed 36,687 inmates and the total area of the KZ was now 338 hectares, including the industrial works. In addition there were a further 20,000 prisoners in outlying camps in Brandenburg and Berlin. Today Sachsenhausen, the site of the former "concentration camp of the German capital" which operated for nine years, has become one of the most important German memorials, and includes compelling exhibitions.

National Socialist City

The politics of architecture

Hitler said himself that he would have rather been an artist than a politician, preferably an architect. Even today, Berlin's many buildings which date from 1933/34 are evidence of this architectural leaning. However when he became Reich Chancellor the "Führer" did not start to redesign the capital city in his own image straightaway. It was in Munich, the "Capital of the (Nazi) Movement" that the first large building contracts were placed by the new government. Just eight weeks after they came to power preparations began for two gigantic Party buildings on Königsplatz and for the "Haus der deutschen Kunst" (House of German Art) by the Englischer Garten. By contrast, the new Reich Chancellor initially held back on any new projects in Berlin. He certainly did not have the "picture of the newly built city of Berlin" in his mind in 1909 when he was in a shelter for the homeless in Vienna, although this is what he told his guests round the dinner table in 1941. Even Goebbels recounted in his diary entries contained in the book "From the Kaiserhof to the Reich Chancellery" published in 1934 that the "Führer" had already thought about a "grandiose remodelling of the German capital" and had all the details ready "in the project stage". However, if this account is compared with Goebbels' original notes it is obvious that, as usual, the Berlin Gauleiter had manipulated his comments later. In reality, the first building projects in Berlin can be traced back to plans made by the city authorities before Hitler came to power and which were frequently associated with job creation, although they were not buildings for general use. The housing programme, which had been halted back in 1931 because of the world economic crisis, did not recover during the peacetime of the Third Reich. Instead, construction workers and raw materials were all concentrated on large prestigious buildings to help promote the Nazis.

In the last months of the Weimar Republic there had been plans to construct a new building for the Reichsbank in Mitte and in February 1933 the city invited tenders from architects. In October demolition was started on the old building between the Spree Canal and Kurstrasse and on 5th May 1934 the NS leadership celebrated the laying of the foundation stone for the first large construction project of the "new era". Today this building, which has hardly

The Reich Air Ministry on Wilhelmstrasse (today the Federal Finance Ministry) was one of the most important official buildings of the Third Reich.

changed at all externally, accommodates the Ministry for Foreign Affairs. Other authorities also started work on some massive new buildings. Goebbels commissioned the erection of an ambitious extension for his Propaganda Ministry and the part which fronts Mauerstrasse is practically in its original condition. In 1937/38, Goebbels also had an office building constructed for his role as Berlin Gauleiter in the strongly communist borough of Friedrichshain – a conscious choice to demonstrate the victory of the NSDAP. Hermann Göring commissioned his personal architect, Ernst Sagebiel, to create "suitable" accommodation for his newly founded Air Ministry, now the Federal Finance Ministry on Wilhlemstrasse. On Fehrbelliner Platz in Wilmersdorf, the German Workers' Front took several years to erect a huge headquarters building and today various authorities reside in the parts which have been preserved. In Grunewald the Reich Employment Office Service had a massive headquarters built (today the Federal Environment Office) and the largest airport the world had ever seen, designed by Ernst Sagebiel, was constructed on the Tempelhof field. Among the most important construction clients was the mighty German Army, the "Reichswehr" (renamed "Wehrmacht" in 1935). Huge administration buildings and barrack complexes were built for them in Tiergarten, Zehlendorf, Spandau and Reinickendorf. Over a hundred new buildings which originate from 1933-39 and still survive today were erected in Berlin by the state. Among them are buildings which have no apparent connection with the Nazi claim to power, like the Russian Orthodox Church in Wilmersdorf, whose interior decoration was paid for out of Goebbels' housekeeping and the Town Hall in Tiergarten.

The most well-known construction, however, would have to be the stadium for the 1936 Olympic Games. Contrary to the myths which have grown up around the huge sporting complex named the "Areal", Albert Speer, who was to become Hitler's personal architect, had no influence on the design of Werner March's original plans. Also, the "Führer" had never intended to shun the Olympic Games at short notice because the buildings were alleged to be too modern. The sober stone façades of the massive oval were actually not sufficiently monumental for him, but Hitler was well aware that this sporting event, with such interna-

Ernst Sagebiel (centre), the architect of Tempelhof Airport, during construction in 1939.

This propagandist presentation of the Olympic Stadium with a Zeppelin demonstrates the way the regime projected itself.

tional recognition, represented a unique opportunity to publicise his regime. In the first two weeks of August 1936 Goebbels and Speer promoted Berlin correspondingly, as a clearly National Socialist city; rows of pompous flags decorated all the important streets, the linden trees on Berlin's most beautiful boulevard had to give way to flag poles and tens of thousands of Berliners hung swastika flags out of their windows. The atmosphere in the capital during the most expensive Olympic Games ever held was really enthusiastic. The Olympic Stadium and the other sporting arenas were packed full on every day and spectators cheered on the winners as much as they did the "Führer". The Reich Chancellor himself proved to be a bad sport; when German athletes were victorious he was seen celebrating on the VIP rostrum, but if they were defeated he gave them a black look. However, even Goebbels could do nothing to stop Jesse Owens, the black US sprinter and winner of four gold medals, from becoming the darling of the public.

Apart from the sports complex itself, it is mainly the Olympic village several kilometres to the west of the stadium outside the city which has been preserved from the 1936 Games. Only just though, because the 150 or so idyllically situated houses have been left empty for decades and are in a visible state of disrepair. It was no coincidence that the accommodation for the male competitors was so far away; after the Olympics they were turned into barracks for the nearby Luftwaffe station of Döberitz. The female athletes, on the other hand, were accommodated on the Reichssportfeld itself.

Contrary to popular belief there is no "typical" Nazi architecture, as the buildings which remain from the thirties demonstrate. Their strictly simple neo-classical style with a lot of large quarry stone blocks and massive window ledges actually followed similar trends to those apparent in Scandinavia and even in the USA. However, the building decoration had particular characteristics; no architect abstained from using eagles in every possible variation, on reliefs composed of swastikas and on friezes or mosaics with themes based on Nazi ideology. In many cases these additions have been removed but if one takes a closer look or searches in parts of the buildings which are not accessible to the public, one can still find traces of the martial decoration – even swastika friezes themselves in a building at 93, Dorotheenstrasse, which is used by the Bundestag.

Megalomaniac visions

The plans for turning Berlin into the "World Capital Germania", designed by Albert Speer, were an intrinsic part of National Socialistic rule, but many myths have grown up around these utterly megalomaniac visions. For example, Hitler did not initially get involved in city planning through any initiative of his own, but because he was asked by the Mayor of Berlin to make a specific decision about the exact route of the underground S Bahn line between Potsdamer Platz and Friedrichstrasse stations. Hitler used this opportunity to demand plans from the city authorities for the new lay-out of the German capital. Their employees accordingly drew up designs for a Nord-Süd-Achse (North-South-Axis) between Spreebogen and Tempelhofer Feld (today, Tempelhof Airport), thereby revisiting the ideas on restructuring the west end of Berlin, which had been under constant discussion for over a century. In addition, a large Ost-West-Achse (East-West-Axis) was to be created, which would link Charlottenburg with Mitte. The first design met with Hitler's basic approval but was considered too modest. He wanted a "huge triumphal arch for the undefeated army of the World War" and a "really large assembly hall capable of holding 250,000 people." However, the planning did not make much progress because the thinking of the architects working for the city authorities was much more restrained (realistic) than that of the "Führer". It wasn't until 1936 that Hitler finally made up his mind to entrust Albert Speer, who was at the time only just 31 years old, with this "largest of all" building contracts. In the meantime his wishes had grown to completely grotesque proportions and the North-South-Axis now had to be 120 metres wide. Over the next few years Speer increased the dimensions further; if one compares the first plans for the Nord-Süd-Achse made in his office in 1936 with the last ones made in 1942 the ever increasing proportions are quite clear. Most of Speer's designs were architecturally banal, consisting mainly of gigantic enlargements of the buildings already created in the thirties. Most of the ground plans were characterised by impractically large halls; the width alone of the Nord-Süd-Achse would have created an intimidating effect. The

Albert Speers' model for the transformation of Berlin into the "World Capital Germania". View of the "Great Hall" through the "Arch of Triumph".

"Grosse Halle" (Great Hall), the most colossal of all the plans, was supposed to have a 250 metre wide dome and reach an overall height of 290 metres. Perhaps with today's technology and unlimited resources such a building could be constructed, but in Speer's times it was technically out of the question. All the quarries in Europe would not have had enough stone for the façades of the buildings planned to line the Nord-Süd-Achse. To solve this problem Himmler and Speer agreed that KZ prisoners should be made to work in brick factories and quarries – proof of the fact that Speer, who successfully promoted himself as a "good Nazi" after 1945, was heavily involved in the crimes of the Third Reich.

Only few of Speer's plans were ever completed and fewer still can be seen today; essentially only the East-West-Axis, the route that runs from Theodor-Heuss-Platz (in those days, Adolf-Hitler-Platz), across Ernst-Reuter-Platz (then "Am Knie"), the Strasse des 17. Juni (Charlottenburger Chaussee) and Unter den Linden, as far as Schlossplatz. By Hitler's 50th birthday on 20th April 1939, the whole route had been widened and furnished with a total of 703 new double street lamps, of which only a few dozen remain today. The Charlottenburger Tor, a double victory gate structure built in 1907/08, had to be moved apart by a few metres. Moving the Siegessäule (Victory Column) from Königsplatz (today,

The new Reich Chancellery in Vossstrasse, Albert Speer's only completed large building.

Platz der Republik) to the Grosser Stern was actually a preparation for the North-South-Axis. So that this symbol of the Prussian victories in the wars of 1864, 1866 and 1870/71 did not appear too small on its new site, which was a much larger expanse, Speer simply had a fourth section of support added to the column. Parts of the planned road tunnel built to prevent traffic jams at the crossroads of the East-West and North-South Axes still remain underground. Only the shell of one building on the planned Nord-Süd-Achse was ever completed: the "Haus des Fremdenverkehrs" (Tourist Centre) on "Runder Platz". It stood roughly where today Potsdamer Strasse passes Hans Scharoun's State Library and in 1964 the ruins of the "Haus des Fremdenverkehrs" were pulled down to make way for this new building. Today, the largest visible legacy of the "Germania Plan" is the Grossbelastungskörper in General-Papen-Strasse. This 32 metre high, 135,000 ton cement construction, with 18 metre deep foundations, was meant to test the weight bearing capacity of the ground.

Lost without trace is Albert Speer's only completed major building in Berlin, which in fact had nothing to do with the "Germania Plan": the new Reich Chancellery. Contrary to Speer's version of events, the 420 metre long building consisting mainly of corridors and halls took longer to plan and construct than just eleven months. Hitler had actually already been intending to erect a new state building for himself on Vossstrasse on the southern edge of the Ministers' Gardens since 1934. Early versions of the finally realised plans put together in Speer's office date from 1935, demolition of the old houses along Vossstrasse started in 1936 and in 1937 the first models of the façades were drawn up. In January 1938, when in his memoirs Speer claims to have first heard of the project, the huge excavations and the foundations already existed. The total cost of the building, which was equipped with all the latest technology available, came to the horrendous sum of 90 million Reichsmark – the equivalent of about one thousand million euros today. The showpiece was the 146 metre long marble gallery leading to Hitler's "office", which was 390 square metres in size and where the dictator received visitors sitting at his desk (which has survived and is incidentally on display at the new permanent

Parade on the Ost-West-Axis (today Strasse des 17. Juni) on 6th June 1939 in honour of the "Legion Condor" who had returned from the Spanish Civil War.

exhibition in the German History Museum in the Zeughaus opened in 2006). However, because the "New Reich Chancellery" was conceived before the "Germania" plans, its massive dimensions soon seemed too small to Hitler and his architect, so Speer designed a new "Führer Palace", with a 500 metre long gallery and a 900 square metre "study". This was going to be situated where the comparatively modest building of the Federal Reich Chancellor - with its 142.5 square metre study - now stands. When the "Germania" project was complete, the new Reich Chancellery was to be used by Hitler's Deputy, Rudolf Hess. It survived the war in a damaged state and was demolished between 1949 and 1951. Some of the marble was used for the construction of the Soviet Memorial in Treptow and Mohrenstrasse U-Bahn station; other fragments were made into a rockscape for monkeys in the Friedrichsfelde Zoo.

"People's Community" and persecution

The prime requisite for Albert Speer's plans to alter Berlin was space. The North-South-Axis itself could actually mainly be built on the area which then still consisted of the railway lines belonging to Potsdamer and

Traffic at a standstill on Potsdamer Platz in Berlin on 27th March 1936, when a minute's silence is inserted into one of Hitler's speeches.

Anhalter stations and which have now been partly turned into parks and are partly unused. But for large buildings, such as Hermann Göring's, "Reichsmarschallamt" (Reich Marshal's Office), which was to be situated along the "Germania's" main boulevard, residential areas housing thousands of Berliners would have to be sacrificed and alternative accommodation would have to be created before any construction work could start. Hitler's architect saw a solution in the regime's race policy; in the minutes of an official discussion on 14th September 1928, it states that "Professor Speer tabled a suggestion which aims to free up the required large blocks of flats by evicting Jews. This suggestion must be treated in strict confidence as Professor Speer first wants to find out the Führer's views. Then the necessary legal machinery would have to be created." Hitler agreed and Speer's colleagues set to work. This memorandum is remarkable because it was written eight weeks before the so-called Reichskristallnacht and is proof that on his own initiative, Speer was actively involved in the persecution of the Jews.

In the National Socialist State there were various concurrent strands of anti-Semitism. There were the "Radau" (rowdy) anti-Semites, mainly members of the SA who took out their prejudices and aggression on a people who were being systematically deprived of their rights. They had often harassed Jews even before 1933 and then later held up and robbed more and more Jewish shops. Julius Streicher's propaganda newspaper "Der Stürmer" published lists of the names and addresses of Jewish owned shops which were then repeatedly looted by the "National Comrades", SA troops, Hitler Youths and just ordinary citizens. The Liechtenstein umbrella shop in Königsstrasse on Alexanderplatz, for example, had three shop window smashed in the space of a few days, about two or three hundred excited people demanded the closure of the Kornblum tie shop and a wild mob in civilian clothes set about looting the "Jewish" Westmann department store in Frankfurter Strasse at five o'clock in the morning – evidently a planned attack.

A second group of anti-Semites had different motives. These were careerists who found that all these anti-Jewish actions a good opportunity to demonstrate their allegiance to the Nazis and they were capable of almost any bureaucratic perfidy. In September 1934, the Mayor of the borough of Tiergarten decreed that the traditional tabernacles could no longer be erected on the Jewish harvest festival - for "building control reasons". On the 19th July 1935, the Berlin city authorities ordered that Jewish run ice-cream parlours had to close at 7 p.m. - which meant that in the high season they were unable to open in the evenings. The borough offices of Steglitz decreed that their employees were forbidden to give any contracts to Jews and were no longer allowed to shop in Jewish shops; they were not even allowed to consult a Jewish doctor or lawyer privately. In 1936 the Regional Employment Court in Berlin made a ruling that if an ("Aryan") employee married a Jewish woman it constituted grounds for dismissal. As from 15th May 1937, any waste material collections could not be sold on to Jewish traders and two weeks later, on 3rd June, Berlin councillors advised on how Jews could gradually be banned from using public bathing facilities. They wanted to pass a central order that would not cause any ramifications abroad. Two indoor baths had already been banned and they put strongly worded anti-Semitic signs on all the other ones apart from the one in Dennewitzstrasse. Local politicians suggested the same thing for the open-air bathing facilities, with the exception of Wannsee, which attracted especially large numbers of foreigners.

Finally, there were the "rational" anti-Semites who despised both the rowdies and the petty bureaucrats because they felt superior to them. The "rational" anti-Semites were mainly to be found in the upper echelons of the administration and in leading positions in the Gestapo, frequently had an academic education and wanted to expel the Jews "cleanly" by systematically withdrawing their basic means of living. To achieve their aim they set up a series of laws to cover the whole of Germany, such as the 1935 "Nuremberg Race Laws", which placed even stricter limits on how Jews could earn money and forced the "Aryanisation" of Jewish property. Speer and his colleagues belonged to this third group.

During the Third Reich the concept of a "National Comrades" was of central importance throughout German society, which of course also included Berlin. It defined the totality of "National Comrades" of German blood and excluded Jews, Sinti and Roma ("gypsies"), homosexuals and all opponents of the regime. After the "Nuremberg race laws" had been passed, the State became responsible exclusively for the welfare of the "People's Community"; all outsiders ("Volksfremde") could and should be exploited for their benefit (and the benefit of the many who took advantage of the system). The NS regime quickly realised that hatred of the Jews, which often resulted in the unleashing of violence, provided an outlet for their supporters. From 1933 onwards these attacks on Jews became a daily occurrence, although they did not affect the lives of Jews in an anonymous city like Berlin as much as those in small towns or especially in the countryside. Many of these Jews, therefore, moved to Berlin and this explains why the official population of the Berlin Jews fell by only 17,000 (from 160,000 to 153,000) despite the fact that over the same period almost 28,000 Jews left the capital to go abroad. Emigration was however not easy; most countries refused to take Jewish refugees – anti-Semitism was not confined to Germany.

The Synagogue in Fasanenstrasse on fire.

The authorities began to put more pressure on the Jews. Many newspapers increased the intensity of their tirades of hate and the police made arbitrary raids on Jewish property. In June 1938 Goebbels stressed to a group of 300 leading officials that: "The watchword is not law, but harassment". Yet even this tougher government line was not sufficient to gain control of the aggression of the thousands of Nazi supporters in Berlin. Goebbels was, therefore, nothing short of grateful when a Jewish youth from Hanover gunned down a German diplomat in Paris on 7th November 1938. After seeking Hitler's approval, the Propaganda Minister ordered his followers to stage a pogrom and the police, fire brigade and Gestapo were told not to intervene. During the night of 9/10 November hordes of SA and Hitler youths marched through the streets breaking shop windows (hence the term "Reichskristallnacht", whose exact derivation is unknown), setting synagogues on fire, destroying Jewish property and beating up Jewish citizens. Helga Narthoff, a Berlin Jewess, described the scene in her diary: "On the Kurfürstendamm display dummies daubed with graffiti lay amongst broken glass. From the windowless shop-fronts tattered clothes fluttered in the breeze. The looters had painted a picture of total destruction and violence. In the shops themselves drawers had been ripped out and thrown to the ground, there were clothes strewn everywhere, shattered furniture, china which had been smashed and kicked to pieces and dented hats." The

Persecuted people seek support for emigration at the "Association for the Aid for Jews" in 1938.

Swiss newspaper Der Bund ran the following report on 11th November: "On the Kurfürstendamm and in the streets nearby, groups of four or five young men, armed with wooden hammers and saws, devastated the Jewish shops. (...) In front of the Jewish grocery stores young people distributed cheese and other goods that they had removed from the shop windows. The crowds looked on in silence." The reaction of the Berliners was mainly actually to play a waiting game; not even the "careerists" or the "rational" Jew haters wanted to identify with the "Rowdy anti-Semites".

The journalist, Ruth Andreas-Friedrich, made this comment about the morning after the pogrom: "The bus conductor looks at me as if he wants to tell me something important, but then he just shakes his head and looks away guiltily. My fellow passengers don't look at me at all. Everyone looks as if they are asking to be forgiven. (...) On the corner of Fasanenstrasse a crowd has built up. It is a silent mass, staring in embarrassment at the synagogue whose dome is shrouded in clouds of smoke. "Damned disgrace", whispers a man next to me. I look at him fondly." The SPD in exile issued the report: "The protest of the population of Berlin was clear. (...) It ranged from a contemptuous look and a gesture of nausea to openly voiced disgust and strong swearwords." But this was usually as far as the protests went. Ruth Andreas-Friedrich remarked self-critically: "We who sit here, who ride on the bus and are dying of shame. Brothers in shame. Comrades in remorse. But if everyone is ashamed, who

Enthusiastic members of the "Federation of German Girls" cheer the "Führer".

actually smashed the glass? It wasn't you and it wasn't me. What's the name of this person, the anonymous stranger?"

There were exceptions to this lack of action which was the main response to the riots. Police Lieutenant Wilhelm Krützfeld, for example, prevented SA men from setting fire to the synagogue in Oranienburgerstrasse (today the Centrum Judaicum); he was officially reprimanded and was forced to take early retirement. Another unnamed policeman also showed a lot of courage; together with an army corporal he protected two Jewish women and their children who were about to be attacked by the Nazi mob in Weinmeisterstrasse in Mitte. However, such bravery was the exception – most Berliners looked in the other direction or at most only vented their disapproval of the pogrom behind closed doors. Ten of the thirty synagogues in Berlin were completely destroyed and a further thirteen were damaged. In addition the SA troops raided at least 60 private prayer rooms, demolished over 1000 shops and killed scores of people. In Berlin alone over 12,000 Jews were arrested and taken to concentration camps. Not only did the Jewish communities have to hand over all their insurance claim money as "reparation" but also pay a billion Reich Marks to the state. After the pogrom a further 30,000 Berlin Jews emigrated – practically everyone who had a chance of escaping abroad.

After the "Reichkristallnacht" everything was "Aryanised" even more ruthlessly, with

"Day of National Work" on 1st May 1936 in the Lustgarten.

the result that Nazi profiteers obtained Jewish property at much less than its true value. All over Germany many small and large fortunes were made in this way and in only very few cases was this injustice put right or appropriate compensation made. In Berlin there are still court cases pending in connection with real estate that was once owned by Jewish Germans – for example those concerning the prime sites of the Wertheim department stores on Potsdamer Platz and Leipziger Platz. This "Aryanisation" had a stabilising effect for the "People's Community"; anyone who could make a profit did so - and then were even less inclined to speak up against the regime. On the whole the Berliners' reaction to the anti-Jewish violence in 1938 was as muted as it had been during the violence against the KPD and the SPD in the spring of 1933. It would be presumptuous to demand heroic deeds from the inhabitants of the capital in those days, but in the decades that followed the war many people were not even prepared to concede that their silence had been at the very least indecent.

Daily Life in the War

Initial scepticism

On 1st September 1939 the atmosphere in the capital was subdued – and not just because the sky was heavy with grey clouds. Joseph Goebbels noted: "People are serious, but composed." On this Friday morning, when Hitler left the Reich Chancellery for the drive to the Kroll Opera House with his usual convoy of black Mercedes limousines, no spontaneous applause broke out along the route as it had done for years when the "Führer and Reich Chancellor" appeared in public for a few moments. After all the triumphs which they had cheered Hitler for, the Berliners now felt afraid; they sensed that the war that Germany had started at 4.45 that morning would change their lives. Yet although there was so little enthusiasm for the attack on Poland (memories of the 1914-1918 World War were still too fresh) there was also very little protest. William L. Shirer, the CBS correspondent in Germany, shared his impressions of the first day of the war in the capital with his listeners in the USA: "Up till now there has been nothing unusual about life on the streets of Berlin except that the radios are turned up to full volume and military music alternating with announcements." Later in his evening broadcast he added: "A few hours ago I went out to eat. My restaurant looked so dark from the outside that I thought it was closed, but after I had passed through the curtained double door I found the inside was brightly lit and full of people. I had no difficulty at all getting a good meal, a glass of Pils and a cup of coffee."

This all changed at 18.55 when suddenly the sirens started to wail. The Berliners were familiar with this piercing sound because the air raid wardens had been constantly staging practice drills. But now, for the first time, the wailing signalled a real raid. "Everyone rushed to their cellars," noted Goebbels. However, no bombs were dropped as yet; the two Polish aircraft heading for Berlin turned away. After just 24 hours the Berliners had already half come to terms with the war. In Shirer's words: "The people seem to be in a better mood today now that they have got through the first night of mandatory darkness, which takes some getting used to. Most of them probably went to bed at about 1 a.m. when it became clear that any possible air raids by planes from Poland would have taken place by then." The city seemed to Shirer to be "completely normal from the outside. The

The swastika flying in front of the Kaiser Wilhelm Memorial Church near the Zoological Garden in 1939.

people were still going to work as usual, although there were far fewer cars on the roads."

On 3rd September it was obvious that Great Britain and France did not intend to give in to Hitler's aggression as they had done on so many previous occasions. According to Albert Speer, who recalled this Sunday in Berlin thirty years later, the Berliners reacted as follows: "The streets remained empty. On Wilhelmplatz there were no crowds shouting for Hitler and in keeping with the desolate mood Hitler had his cases packed into cars and left for the front." The atmosphere did not improve over the next few days. Reports of the Wehrmacht's advances in Poland were so euphoric that they were often dismissed as pure propaganda. Instead, rumours spread that in Poland over 60,000 German soldiers had been killed and twice as many again had been wounded. Even Poland's capitulation at the end of September was not greeted with any enthusiasm for war. George F. Kennan, then an American diplomat at the embassy on Pariser Platz (on the exact spot where the future US Embassy is currently being built) wrote in his diary: "The Berliners themselves – I mean the ordinary people – were the least infected by Nazism. (…) I can vouch for the fact that during the victory parade held to celebrate the end of the Polish Campaign they just stood there in restrained, sullen silence." Most Germans were still expecting that the western powers would soon launch an attack; although this initial scepticism proved to be exaggerated for the majority of Berliners.

Proud normality

The October of 1939 brought wonderful sunny early autumn weather, but no French bomber aircraft or enemy tanks or soldiers. The tense, nervous mood in Berlin changed – into one of pride. On 11th October the rumour spread that the British Prime Minister had been brought down. In a tough speech delivered on 3rd September Neville Chamberlain had (rhetorically speaking) put Hitler in his place and declared war until the rights of peoples had been restored. The Herald Tribune correspondent reported that when they heard this rumour (which had no truth in it) Berlin market women "threw cabbages around for joy". When the first victorious Wehrmacht units returned from Poland, an SS news agency recorded in a top secret report that they were fêted, "with great enthusiasm by the population almost everywhere in Berlin". Anxiety about the war had been dispelled. In mid-December, William Shirer told his listeners: "Walking through the streets of Berlin on this beautiful Saturday morning it is difficult to imagine that a World War is going on." The young American journalist, Howard K. Smith, who took up his post as a correspondent in the capital on 1st January 1940, had the same impression: "From inside Berlin the war was unreal. It was as if it was an event happening on another planet." Shortly after the Wehrmacht attack on Denmark and Norway at the beginning of April 1940, a Berlin contact of the SPD in exile reported: "An atmosphere of optimism about the outcome of the war has developed. The thought just doesn't occur to most people that Germany could lose this war." On 20th April on the "Führer's birthday" there

On 6th July 1940 after the victory of the Wehrmacht over France, Hitler is at the height of his powers. The Berliners frenetically celebrate his return from the front.

were thousands standing on Wilhelmplatz again, cheering Hitler. At the beginning of May, Shirer gave this description of the attitude of the Berliners: "It would be difficult to exaggerate the feeling of triumph that prevails in the Third Reich today." The German attack on France, Belgium and the Netherlands on 10th May only briefly halted this euphoria; by the beginning of June, when German tanks were just outside Paris, Shirer reported that things were back to normal in Berlin: "Today, on Sunday – it was warm and sunny – everyone who is still in Berlin seemed to be taking a trip to the forests or the lakes nearby because the atmosphere was so peaceful and quiet." This mood reached its climax on 6th July. Following the capitulation of the "arch enemy", France, Hitler arrived at Anhalter Station in his special train and at the peak of his power. Literally hundreds of thousands of enthusiastic Berliners lined the streets along the short route to the new Reich Chancellery. Goebbels wrote, for once totally accurately: "At two o'clock Wilhelmsplatz is teeming with people. Everyone is waiting for the Führer. Above them is the wonderful July sunshine. A real day of celebration. (...) The streets are strewn with flowers and look like a multi-coloured carpet." Private film footage confirms this description by Goebbels; the Berliners were genuinely celebrating. This was not orchestrated enthusiasm.

Not even the British air attacks on the capital which started at the end of August 1940 changed things. Peter Jung, who was seven years old at the time, recalled later: "The first bombed houses excited a lot of curiosity. I can remember my mother taking me to Lüneburger Strasse in Moabit to look at a house which had been hit by bombs." Soon, however, it became clear what the war in the air was going to mean for the capital. After the first few deaths in the capital William Shirer wrote in his diary: "The Berliners are devastated. They had not imagined that anything like this could happen." Goebbels noted: "Now Berlin is directly involved in the war. It's a good thing." Hitler interrupted his summer sojourn in the "Berghof" near Berchtesgaden and returned to Berlin. His Propaganda Minister commented: "The Führer wants to be in Berlin while the bombing is going on." This was relatively safe because back in 1935/36 Hitler had had a huge air raid shelter built beneath the banqueting hall of the Reich Chancellery palace. With a ceiling 1.6 metres thick it was, in those days, absolutely bomb-proof. Some other bunkers had also been built, for example under the Air Ministry and in the foundations of the new Reich Chancellery. Despite seven years of permanent propaganda about anti-aircraft defence the Berlin population mostly had just makeshift propped-up cellars as protection. In his angry reaction to the British bombing of the German capital, Hitler not only ordered an even stronger attack on London (in fact, in 1940 ten times as many Londoners were killed as Berliners) but also a massive bunker building programme. For the latter he made Albert Speer responsible, who was anything but enthusiastic about this unglamorous task.

The anti-aircraft tower in the zoo was one of the largest shelters for the population during the Allied attacks.

Living with the bombing

In the autumn and winter of 1940 the air raid sirens wailed more or less every other night in Berlin. The first important cultural buildings to be hit were the Berlin Cathedral on the Lustgarten and Museum Island. The number of civilian victims rose slowly but surely and it wasn't long before over

Berlin women after an air-raid in front of the large Zoo bunker. Prams have to be left in front of the entrance.

10,000 Berliners had lost their homes. There was no hope of any rebuilding; all resources were being used for the bunker programme. In the space of only a few weeks and months dozens of shelters made of reinforced concrete several metres thick were erected; some of them were quite small for only a few hundred people and there were also huge fortresses, the so-called "Flakturmpaare" (pairs of anti-aircraft towers) in three Berlin parks. Only the impressive ruin of the former gun turret in Humboldthain is still accessible today; the pair of anti-aircraft towers in the Zoological Garden have completely disappeared and of those in Frierichshain Volkspark there only remain a few dangerous artificial caves beneath a mound of rubble. These six concrete giants, based on an idea of Hitler's, were actually meant to be an effective defence against the bombing raids on the city centre but this proved to be a total miscalculation. Nevertheless, the anti-aircraft towers served a purpose – during each of the worst bombing raids they provided total protection for more than 35,000 Berliners. Any other measures taken by the government were of a cosmetic nature. For example, wooden scaffolding was erected around the Victory Column on the Grosser Stern and camouflage nets hung above Pariser Platz and Charlottenburger Chaussee (today Strasse des 17. Juni). In this way Berlin landmarks that were easily recognisable from the air were meant to be disguised and thus make the Royal Air Force (RAF) target bombing on the capital more difficult. In the spring of 1941 the British attacks continued with increasing intensity and the State Opera House on Unter den Linden was the first public building to be totally gutted. The reaction among the Berliners was varied. The 23 year old Russian exile, Marie "Missie" Wassiltschikow recorded in her diary: "Air-raid. My fear of them is growing. Now my heart starts to thump as soon as I hear the sirens start wailing." On the other hand, architects working on the "Germania" plans in Speer's office cynically viewed the destruction caused by bombing as "valuable preparation for the purposes of reconstruction".

In 1941 the Berliners made an effort to keep the daily routine going. The theatres, cinemas, bars and restaurants continued to open, even if they had less on offer and

Goebbels makes a speech in the Berlin Philharmonic Hall on the occasion of Hitler's 54th birthday on 20th April 1943

going out for a meal required rationing stamps as well as money. More and more women were working extra shifts in the factories, but this was not enough to make up for the loss of hundreds of thousands of young men who had been drafted into the Wehrmacht and the requirement for fighting troops as reinforcements, especially in the ammunition factories. There were numerous important armament industry works in and around Berlin, including large factories such as the electronics companies of Siemens (in Siemensstadt) and Telefunken (on Platz des 4. Juli in Lichterfelde), the railway works of Borsig in Wedding (which had mainly switched to tank production) and in Oranienburg, to the north of Berlin, the aircraft factories run by Heinkel. Almost as important were the hundreds of medium-sized suppliers in the so-called export district along Ritterstrasse in Kreuzberg, where vital parts for engines, radar equipment and fuses were produced. By 1941 a forced labour system had increasingly proliferated both in Berlin and throughout Germany. This initially involved prisoners of war and German Jews but soon drafted in East and West Europeans "called up for essential service". Six twelve-hour shifts a week was the norm; some groups of forced labourers had to work even longer.

The Berliners experienced several changes of heart in the autumn months of 1941. There was an atmosphere of hope fol-

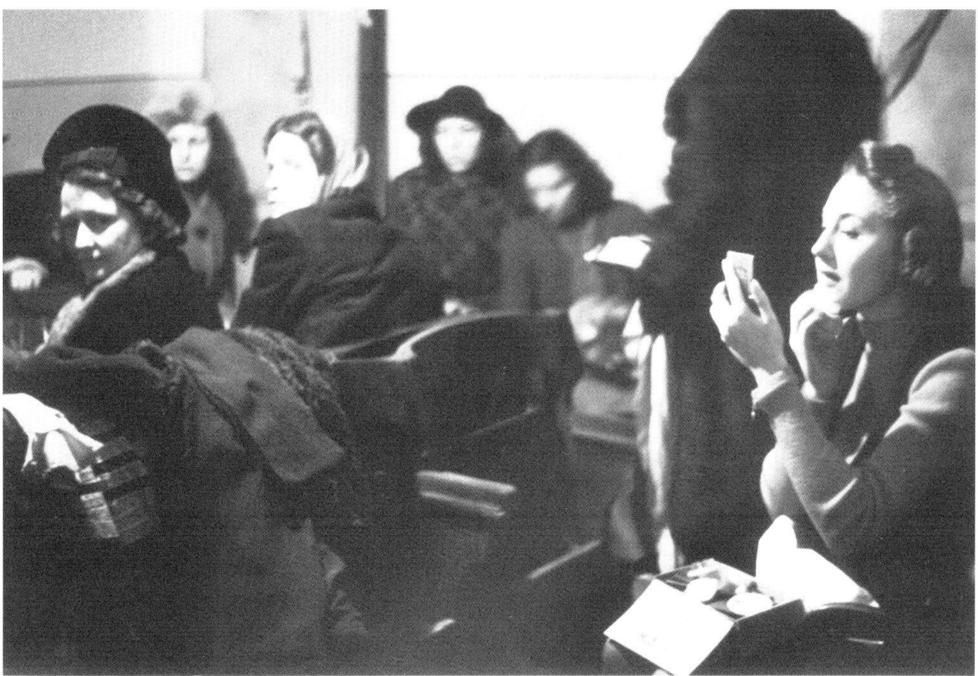

In the underground air-raid shelter of the German Opera House (Deutsche Oper) in Charlottenburg in 1943.

lowing the Wehrmacht victories during their attack on the Soviet Union on 22nd June 1941 and then worry and fear darkened the mood. From Berlin the observant SS information service, whose top secret reports were in essence reliable, reported a widespread feeling that the war was going in England's favour. This was compounded by the noticeable pressure caused by continued British bombing. US correspondent Smith recalled: "In the morning after an air attack people were in a terrible state after a sleepless night of nervous tension. If a bombing raid started in the early morning or lasted until after sunrise, the traffic came to a standstill and the Berlin working day was thrown into chaos until at least lunchtime." Nearly all Berliners permanently lived with the likelihood of having to get up during the night, grab their "air-raid luggage" packed with their most important possessions and papers and rush to the cellar or bunker. However, the British could not keep up this pressure on the capital and after two further series of minor raids on the capital in August and September the RAF turned their attention to other targets. Between 30th September 1941 and 15th January 1943 there were only eleven air-raid alarms in the capital, mainly false ones. Life in Berlin went back to normal again – for the last time.

An NSDAP official and a wounded Hitler Youth at the beginning of 1944 after an air-raid on Lehniner Platz in Wilmersdorf.

Transportation to death

It is not clear exactly when the decision was made to murder all Jews living in the Third Reich. Most of the evidence points to the second half of 1941. In the course of these months the Nazi authorities issued orders for a series of measures to be carried out which made life more difficult for the Jews. At the beginning of August Jewish men between the ages of 18 and 45 were forbidden to leave the country. About 64,700 professed Jews were living in Berlin at this time (73,800 according to the "Race" guidelines of the Nazi regime). A good 28,000 of them had to work in inhumane conditions as forced labourers; the rest were either too young or too old. From 19th September 1941 Jews had to wear a scrap of cloth stamped with two yellow crossed over triangles, "securely sewed on" and "visible on the left chest of the clothing" – the notorious "yellow star" which, incidentally, the wearers had to purchase themselves at a cost of 10 Pfennig each. These labels simplified any further tightening of the anti-Jewish measures. Anyone wearing the star was not allowed to use the trams, couldn't buy a newspaper or make calls from a public telephone. Howard K. Smith thought that the introduction of the yellow star in Berlin was, at least in the first few days, a "colossal failure". A few months later he wrote that, "on the first day that "Aryan" Germans met a Jew wearing his radiant yellow star, they lowered their heads – it was really remarkable how they all reacted in the same way." However this possibly honest reaction, observed by many other eye-witnesses, did not stop thousands of Berliners from making a personal profit out of the suffering of their persecuted fellow citizens. After Albert Speer issued an order for the "clearance of Jews' homes", there were auctions selling off the contents of Jewish households. Smith went along to some of them: "The Aryans there fought like jackals round a cadaver over a few pathetic things that were in short supply because of the war in Russia. The government still achieved a good price for this old stuff because the auctioneers had to work with the secret police sitting in the back rows and pushing up the prices." People who were driven out of their homes were often forced to live in "Jews' houses". These were completely over-

These Berliners survive more heavy bombing on Berlin's city centre.

crowded, mostly poorly equipped houses with flats for several families. They belonged to Jews but no "Aryaniser" had yet appropriated them. In such buildings often three or more families lived in each flat. The Jews who were still able to live in their own homes had to put yellow stars on the door so that "People's comrades" could be "warned".

From mid-October the number of such "favourable opportunities" to buy additional household goods increased dramatically. The first "resettlements" to the east also began, which, perfidiously, the Jewish community in Berlin partly had to organise for themselves. On 18th October 1941 the first transport train with 1,013 people on board, left the capital for Lodz (then "Litzmannstadt"). Once there, the deported Berliners were incarcerated in the already overcrowded ghetto with the occupants of 19 other deportation trains from all over the Third Reich, including three more from Berlin. These trains usually consisted of twenty old third class carriages. The Jews who were to be deported had to assemble in collection camps, mainly in the former synagogue in Levetzowstrasse or in the former Jewish old peoples' home in the Grosser Hamburger Strasse (Mitte). The conditions there were ghastly, despite the best efforts of the community. People were often then taken at night, but also in daylight, to the goods stations of Grunewald (Wilmersdorf) or Pulitzstrasse, either by lorry or on foot. There they had to board trains which would take them to an uncertain future. In the 1980s and 90s memorials were erected in all these four locations in remembrance of the fate of over 50,000 Jews deported from Berlin. Practically all of them sooner or later landed up in the death camps "in the east", sometimes via various other intermediate places. The first Berlin Jews who were killed immediately on arrival died in an old fort near the Lithuanian town of Kauna. The last transport train left Berlin for Theresienstadt on 27th March 1945 – by this time the death camp of Auschwitz-Birkenau had already been freed for two months.

The deportations were organised mainly in the "Jews Department" of the "Reich Security Headquarters" run by Adolf Eichmann, which had its central office at 116, Kurfürstenstrasse (Tiergarten). Today, no traces of this building remain, but a bus shelter "turned into" a memorial recalls its history. The most important decisions, however, were made in the district between Wilhelmstrasse, Prinz-Albrecht-Strasse and Anhalter Bahnhof (Kreuzberg). In this headquarters of the SS-State, containing more than a dozen buildings, sat not only SS boss, Heinrich Himmler, but also his notorious colleagues, Reinhard Heydrich, Ernst Kaltenbrunner and Heinrich Müller. The site has been covered with rubble for the past 60 years, but by 2008 the Berlin Senate intends to erect a museum for the Foundation for the Topography of Terror which now currently just runs an open-air exhibition.

Historians still dispute the significance of the Conference on the Wannsee on 20th January 1942 which SS Obergruppenführer Heydrich held in the luxurious villa at 56-58 Am Grossen Wannsee. One can state with certainty that the "final solution to the question of the Jews" was not decided here, because the Holocaust had started long before this date. Heydrich probably wanted to make a special show of his ability to issue directives in front of representatives from other authorities. A completely new exhibition dealing with the conference and the murder of six million European Jews opened in the villa at the beginning of 2006. On the other hand, the decision to commit mass murder was not taken on the site of the present central national "Monument for the murdered Jews of Europe" (generally referred as "The Holocaust Memorial") to the south of the Brandenburg Gate. The memorial's 2,711 wave-shaped concrete steles today stand where for over two hundred years were the former gardens of the Adelspalais, later used as government ministries. Although it's true that Propaganda Minister Goebbels had a private air-raid bunker built there, next to his expensively furnished official home (which still lies under the ground in the north-east corner of Peter Eisenmann's memorial), no decisions about the deportations were made there. Goebbels had always pressed for the removal of all Jews ("Entjudung") from Berlin but was unable to develop any real influence over the SS.

At the end of February 1943 the Gestapo arrested in Berlin, as they did all over the Third Reich, any Jews they could get hold of and "concentrated" them into various collection camps. As the forced labourers were apprehended in armament factories, these waves of arrests are called "Factory Action". At the same time 2,000 Jewish men with "Aryan" wives were taken away, separated from their fellow-sufferers and herded together at 2-4, Rosenstrasse (Mitte). From among their numbers the Gestapo recruited workers for the various Jewish institutions to replace the so-called "Full Jews" who had been deported. A few dozen, perhaps even over a hundred women assembled in front of the expropriated building of the former Social Administration of the Jewish Community. It was a widely-held view that their protests led to the mens' release and today, in memory of their demonstration, a sculpture of figures stands where the building used to be. However, the Gestapo had never intended to deport the "Aryan interrelated" Jews who were being detained in Rosenstrasse - the Nazi regime feared that this may throw the population into "uncertainy" in the middle of the war. Therefore the undoubtedly courageous action by the women did not lead to the release of the men in Rosenstrasse and cannot be used as evidence that the Berliners could have prevented the Holocaust. Since the anti-Jewish measures of 1933-38 had not really led to any decisive reaction on the part of the "Aryan" population and many Berliners had, on the contrary, even profited from the misfortune of their fellow Jewish citizens, there was nothing that could now stand in the way of the murderous machinery of the Holocaust.

From spring 1943 bomb damage becomes part of everyday life in Berlin.

Gradual Destruction

The air battle for Berlin

Only once in Berlin during the war was there mention of the idea that the nightly bombing raids could have something to do with the anti-Jewish policies. On 3rd March 1943, the 32 year old journalist, Ursula von Kardoff, who had remained an independent spirit, noted in her diary: "All over Berlin the rumour that this attack is the reaction to the Jewish transportations." There were actually only just 60 hours between the "Factory action" and the heaviest RAF bombing experienced so far, but in reality there was no connection; it was just pure coincidence.

The heavy attack by 251 bombers was the beginning of the systematic destruction of the capital from the air. Goebbels was visibly shaken when he dictated to his secretary: "There are a huge number of bomb sites. Industrial plants and government buildings have been badly hit as well. The Hedwig Cathedral has been completely gutted by fire, along with four other churches, many hospitals, old peoples' homes etc." The SS news service issued a top secret announcement: "It is being repeatedly said that the English have air superiority, the German Luftwaffe is currently "powerless" and has no way of taking appropriate revenge." Yet the result that Vice Air Marshal Arthur Harris had been striving for - the collapse of morale on the home front – had by no means been achieved. Goebbels very appropriately noted that: "Nobody need think that the Berlin population isn't up to coping with a massive air attack." Ursula von Kardorff had the same impression: "The catastrophes befalling Nazis and anti-Nazis in equal measure are welding the people together." With his concept of "morale bombing" Harris therefore achieved exactly the opposite of his actual aim. The "People's community" had been stabilised and the NSDAP had a task which made them more popular than ever before – they organised "Soforthilfe" ("immediate aid") providing the people who had been bombed out of their homes with food, modest relief accommodation and the necessities of life.

The RAF, however, did not understand all this. Instead, Arthur Harris planned a great onslaught against German morale: "We can devastate Berlin completely if the Americans join in. It will cost us four or five hundred aircraft but it will cost Germany the war." This was the justification he used to get permission to put his plan into action and on 18th November 1943 the "Air

The Hotel "Excelsior" in Kreuzberg was badly hit in February 1945. In the foreground is a woman with her "air-raid luggage".

Battle for Berlin" began; initially with 440 bombers, then four days later a series of three huge air-raids within 72 hours using a total of almost 1600 aircraft. The Berliners experienced a kind of Apocalypse. Ursula von Kardoff described the attacks as "hell", the Norwegian correspondent Theo Findahl reported a "strange oppressive atmosphere of downfall" and Goebbels was so affected that for a few days he didn't even dictate the entries for his diary. But still the prolonged air-raids failed to achieve their real aim. In Berlin, unlike in Hamburg at the end of July/beginning of August 1943, the inner city area was not devastated by a firestorm. This phenomenon only occurred in the Hansa district on the north-west edge of the Tiergarten where barely a dozen of the old three-storey townhouses survived the destructive force of the fires caused by the air-raids. Bombs also rained mercilessly on the old town centre of Charlottenburg, yet still the German capital withstood the enormous force of the attacks with relatively few victims – in November 1943 4,000 people died, a tenth of the deaths in the Hamburg firestorm. The reason for this had mainly to do with the structure of the city; Berlin did not have a medieval city centre with narrow streets full of timber-framed houses which quickly caught fire when bombed from the air, but consisted mostly of buildings with solid walls, broad streets and numerous parks as well as wide expanses of water.

The worst air-raid of the war on 3rd February in 1945 devastates the whole inner city area; here people who have been bombed out of their homes near Anhalter Station.

The RAF gradually continued the destruction. When Harris had to interrupt the bombing at the end of March 1944 the Allies had lost over 600 bombers and almost 3,500 men. In Berlin about 9,000 people had died and 812,000 were homeless. The concentrated large raids were then replaced by constant smaller attacks accompanied by individual mass daylight raids by US bombers which were now being used against the capital for the first time. In 1944 the air sirens wailed on average every three days and the Berliners were being increasingly worn down.

Persecution and resistance

After the mass deportations of spring 1943, there were only about 9,000 Jews left living in Berlin. Between August 1943 and April 1945 a further 25 transport trains left for "the east", but the Gestapo had only been able to arrest about a further one thousand people to send to their deaths. The remainder were "Aryan interrelated", which meant that according to the Nazi "Race Laws" they were married to "non-Jews". A further 1400 people had successfully managed to go into hiding. This was easier to do in the chaos of war than in peacetime, but when food was short it was more difficult to survive. Those who managed to escape persecution mainly hid in garden allotments or in the cellars of houses destroyed by bombs. A few thousand Berliners were kind enough to give these people food and others took payment for it, but anyone who was betrayed had to face the death penalty.

The Nazi regime had already put a stop to public criticism of the persecution of the Jews at the start of the war and thanks to informers lots of remarks made in private had reached the ears of the Gestapo – often with murderous consequences. The Protestant priest Heinrich Grüber and the Catholic Dean Bernhard Lichtenberg for example, had intervened energetically on

On the morning of 21st July 1944 SS units occupied the Bendlerblock in Tiergarten. It was here on the previous day that Graf Stauffenberg's attempted coup had failed.

The resistance fighter Helmuth James Graf von Moltke, the leader of the "Kreisauer Kreis" in front of the People's Court on 10th January 1945.

behalf of the Jews. Both were arrested; Grüber survived two and a half years in a concentration camp but Lichtenberg, who was older, died in 1943 being transported from prison to Dachau concentration camp. Today Lichtenberg has a special chapel dedicated to his memory in the newly built St. Hedwig's Cathedral (Mitte) and there are several plaques commemorating Grüber. In Berlin there are a total of over a thousand memorial stones, monuments and plaques and that's not including the hundreds of "Stolpersteine" ("stumbling stones") which the Cologne artist Günter Demnig has been putting into the pavements since 1997. The small bronze-coloured rectangular blocks are in memory of the victims of the Nazi regime who lived in these streets until they were arrested and murdered.

Of course more of these victims came from the capital than from any other German city. Alongside the 50,000 Berlin Jews who were deported to ghettos or death camps many other Berliners suffered and died; at least 30,000 Communists and Social Democrats, several thousand oppressed Sinti and Roma (Gypsies), about 3,000 as victims of the Nazi "Euthanasia" programme and innumerable homosexuals, Jehovah's Witnesses (then known as "serious bible researchers") and "asocial" citizens. The 80,000 Berlin Jews who emigrated before 1939 must also be added to this list. However, at least ninety per cent of the Berliners lived without having any trouble with Hitler's regime and were not persecuted by the Gestapo, the SS or the police. For them it was the terrible air-raids that killed about 20,000 people, which had the worst effect on their lives.

There were many small resistance groups in Berlin, as there were all over the Third Reich. The most numerous were in former communist or social democratic circles, and also within the church. No-one knows exact numbers but there is nothing to suggest that resistance in the capital was any stronger than, say, in the large industrial towns of the Ruhr. In Berlin, however, resistance took a particular national form which was not linked to its role as a city but more to its function as the seat of government. Practically every conservative and liberal resistance group had its focal point here; one of the few exceptions was the "Weisse Rose" (White Rose) in Munich. The military opposition prepared their coups d'état in the government ministries and general staffs in Berlin and it was also in Berlin that the "Abwehr" ("Defence"), the most significant of the anti-Hitler movements, was active in the secret service of the German Army, although it was not actually "Berlin resistance". Their most promising attempt to oust Hitler finally failed on 20th July 1944. In Tiergarten there is a memorial dedicated to all German resistance against the Hitler regime and part of it includes the rooms in which Colonel Klaus von Stauffenberg, leader of the conspirators and would-be assassinator, gave his orders. Most of those involved and their supporters were sentenced to death in the building which was substituting as the People's Court in Kleistpark in Schöneberg and were then murdered at Plötzensee execution site (Charlottenburg).

Prior to the formation of the military resistance there was a group the Gestapo called "Rote Kapelle" (Red Band) which was peculiar to Berlin. This network of almost 200 government workers, artists and writers, who could loosely be described as friends, was crushed in 1942 and at least 57 of them had to pay for their fight against Hitler with their lives. Numerous memorial plaques, several streets and schools bear their names; for example, Adam Kuckhoff, Harro Schulze-Boysen and his wife Libertas, Arvid and Mildred Harnack as well as Robert Havemann who survived persecution by the Nazis and was put under house arrest two decades later by the GDR Stasi. Another well-known Berlin resistance group was Herbert Baum and his friends; a circle consisting mainly of young Berlin Jews and some Communists who had gone into hiding in the capital. On 18th May 1942 members of the "Gruppe Baum" set fire to "The Soviet Paradise", a propagandist exhibition in the Berlin Lustgarten – although without much success as the show was able to re-open the following day. The Gestapo had infiltrated the group and was able to arrest 54 of them, twenty of whom were executed and Himmler also had more Jews murdered as "reprisals". Among the memorials to the Baum group there is a monument dating back to GDR times in the Lustgarten and a commemorative stone in the Jewish cemetery at Weissensee.

The final battle

When the conspiracy against Hitler failed, allied troops were not yet on German soil, although the British and Americans had gained air supremacy over the entire Third Reich. In 1944 and 1945 they more or less attacked any targets they felt worth bombing and in Berlin the situation became increasingly chaotic. The emergency accommodation could hardly keep up with the extent of the destruction caused by the bombing, food was often unavailable, even with a ration card and there was frequently no gas, water or electricity. At the beginning of 1945 the air-raid sirens wailed every day, sometimes several times as smaller RAF sorties were supplemented by larger air raids by US bombers. In the summer of 1943 Goebbels had actually arranged for the evacuation of children to the country areas outside the city where they would be safe from the bombing, but there were still between up to two and a half million people who had to stay in Berlin in view of its importance as an administrative and industrial centre.

Air Marshal Harris returned to his idea of deciding the war with a massive air-raid on Berlin; he wanted to send in every single British and American plane and attack the capital for four nights and three days, using a total of 20,000 tons of bombs. The US Air Force turned this plan down and instead, on 3rd February 1945, they staged the biggest raid of the Second World War; over a thousand aircraft appeared on the radar screens of the Berlin air defence and their target was the government district. The explosions and fires destroyed most of the southern Friedrichsstadt and Kreuzberg and completely obliterated the newspaper district in and around Kochstrasse. Ursula von Kardoff noted: "Today the city centre experienced its heaviest attack ever. I would never have thought that such intensification were possible." The Washington Post remarked with pride: "In this war no target has ever been saturated with bombs like this." However this newspaper overestimated the results of the bombing; there were not up to 25,000 victims - only 3,000 Berliners died. It was finally obvious that the Third Reich was not going to be forced to its knees from the air.

The Second World War ended on the ground, in the city where Hitler had once wanted to build his "Weltstadt Germania". At the beginning of February 1945 Goebbels, still Gauleiter of Berlin, had already declared the capital as a "fortress". Preparations were now made for a street battle, which in view of the superiority of the Allies, both in numbers and equipment, was doomed from the start. Hitler had been in Berlin since the middle of January, in the Führerbunker beneath the garden of the Reichskanzler-Palais, to be precise. In 1943/44 a mighty air raid shelter had hastily been built here for him, with ceilings four metres thick. As well as Hitler, Goebbels, Speer and the Army Chiefs had

In February 1945 thousands of children are evacuated from Berlin – there are no longer sufficient schools in the Reich capital.

Elderly men, members of the "Volksturm" erect tank barriers out of old trams in March 1945 – preparations for the street battle for the capital.

a safe haven here, unlike the rest of the Berliners who with every wail of the sirens had to fight for a place in the thousand or so public bunkers now in existence, but which could only offer protection to a part of the population.

At the same time the Berliners remaining in the shattered capital were aware that the Soviet tanks were steadily and irresistibly getting nearer. Since the middle of February they had been positioned on the river Oder, less than 60 kilometres from Berlin. Their final offensive began on 16th April 1945 and was more horrifying than the horrors of any battle so far in this war. Four days later the first tanks of the Red Army reached the eastern borders of the city and within a week Berlin was surrounded. Streets full of houses which had so far escaped damage fell victim to the senseless heroism of the German defenders and fire power of the Soviet canons. Particularly hard hit were the Ost-West-Magistralen, broad avenues running from east to west which were part of a road system built in the 1920s. This is why there are hardly any old buildings left along the Frankfurter and Landsberger Allees.

It was only a question of days before the government district in the centre of Berlin would be taken. On the afternoon of 30th April 1945 when Hitler's Reich, which had once stretched from the suburbs of Moscow to the French Atlantic coast, was about the size of the Vatican City, the once popular dictator took his own life in the Führerbunker. Outside his concrete cave the battle

BERLINER MORGENPOST

Reichsminister Dr. Goebbels an die Berliner Bevölkerung

Berlin ist zum Entscheidungskampf angetreten
Die Reichshauptstadt unter dem Gesetz der Front

Der neue Mongolensturm muß sich an unseren Mauern brechen
Der Kampf geht für Freiheit und Zukunft, für unsere Frauen und Kinder

Einführung des Alarmsignals „Feindalarm"

Berliner Notprogramm in Kraft gesetzt

Die Stunde der Bewährung ist da

When Soviet tanks are already lined up on the outskirts of the city, Goebbels calls for the "deciding battle" on 22nd April 1945.

Abschrift Kommandosache!
Marinenachrichtendienst
2010 1952/29/ag1
Fernschreiben von Bachstelze 13 Grau 2 a FRR
FRR
Gen.Oberst Jodl (Zeppelin):
Es ist mir sofort zu melden:
1) Wo sind die Spitzen von Wenck?
2) Wann greifen sie an?
3) Wo ist die 9. Armee?
4) Wohin bricht die 9. Armee durch?
5) Wo sind die Spitzen von Holste?
Adolf Hitler
Verteiler: 1. Skl, 4. Skl., FTO, Adj.Ob.d.M.
1. Skl. B.Nr. 9735/45 Gkdos
Verteiler: Pr.Nr. 1 = Chef Skl
2 = + 1/Skl
3 = I a
An I f
an I b

Hitler's last order from the Führerbunker on 29th April 1945. About thirty hours later the "Führer" committed suicide.

raged on for a further 40 bloody hours; no-one knows exactly how many victims this last of all battles claimed but several thousand Red Army soldiers died just in the storming of the Reichstag building, which Stalin had singled out as a symbolic target. On the morning of 2nd May 1945 the last Garrison Commander of Berlin, General Helmuth Weidling, surrendered to the Soviets with this remarkable order to the few thousand remaining troops: "On 30th April the Führer took his own life and with this action he has abandoned all those who swore loyalty to him. Every hour that you continue to fight is prolonging the terrible suffering of the civilian population of Berlin and the wounded among us. Anyone who now dies in the battle is making a pointless sacrifice." Yet on 3rd May, a few German tanks along with thousands of people tried to break through to the west over the Brunsbüttler Damm in Spandau, in the hope of being able to give themselves up to the Americans at the Elbe. They were shot down mercilessly by the far superior Soviet forces and it wasn't until the 4th May 1945 that there was a ceasefire in the German capital.

Keeping alive

The desperate bid to escape was not unfounded; there was real fear of retribution and the advance of the Red Army brought with it a wave of atrocities, both en route to Berlin and in its conquest. Countless Soviet soldiers raped, looted and murdered. There are no official statistics on these crimes but the number of Berlin women who were raped probably runs into hundreds of thousands.

The fall of Berlin marked the end of the most brutal regime that Europe has ever known. The total surrender of the Wehrmacht on 8th May 1945 also brought free-

In this staged photo dating from 3rd May 1945, Red Army soldiers hoist their flag on the Reichstag building.

dom for countless prisoners and was a release for all those living in what later became West Germany. For Germans living east of the Elbe and in Berlin this was only true to a certain extent; for them the end of the war meant that the constant threat of death from bombs or grenades had been removed, but they didn't gain real freedom in 1945 because as soon as General Weidling surrendered, their new masters started to build up their power base. Led by Walter Ulbricht, a group of ten communists who had just returned from exile in the Soviet Union drove in convoy into the shattered city from their quarters in the Brandenburg village of Bruchmühle. Their job was to select Berliners considered as "trustworthy" by the Soviet authorities to perform civil functions. This not only facilitated the task of the occupying forces of the Red Army but also cemented the communist claim to power. Ulbricht issued a clear directive from Bruchmühle: "It must look democratic but we must ensure that we have everything under our control."

The Berliners had nothing to offer in the way of resistance and in any case they were too preoccupied with organising their own survival. It was actually quite surprising how quickly rudimentary public services were re-established during the first couple of months when the city was occupied exclusively by the Red Army. The Soviet Commandant, General Nikolaj Bersarin, did his best to get the city infrastructure working again. The Berliners were set to work for hours or days at a time clearing all the main streets of rubble and Bersarin's Officers at last managed to bring their marauding soldiers under control. From mid-May 1945 the number of crimes against women decreased substantially, as did the violent lootings. The first post-war Berlin newspaper, Die Tägliche Rundschau, was also published at this time under the auspices of the Red Army.

The devastation in the German capital was enormous. 8,500 hospital beds remained out of an original 39,000; only half the bridges were still passable – and practically none at all in the city centre. Most of the underground network was under water and 25 kilometres of tunnels between Wedding station in the north and Gneisenaustrasse in the south and Potsdamer Platz in the west and Frankfurter

Allee in the east were actually flooded. One in three homes had been totally destroyed and many of the rest were badly damaged. Food provision had completely broken down and it was mid-May before the Soviet authorities managed to get supplies through to Berlin. At the end of May new ration cards were finally issued and these were to remain in use for several years to come.

On 13th May, just eleven days after surrender and nine days after the end of the last battles worth mentioning, the first official football game took place in Berlin; a football pitch in Weissensee was cleared and a German team consisting of older players from local clubs took on a team of Red Army soldiers. On the same day Berlin's cultural life started its post-war history; the Berlin Chamber Orchestra gave its first concert in the Bürgersaal ("Citizens' Hall") of the Schöneberg Town Hall. In June the first cafés opened on the Kurfürstendamm – in retrospect this seems almost incredible, but there are photos and film clips to prove it.

However, this surprising normality hardly features at all in the memoirs of those who lived through these times. They do not recall pictures of young women in summer dresses strolling through the ruins of Tauentzienstrasse in the sunshine after the end of the battles. These scenes were exceptions which were not typical of the Berlin summer of 1945 but they demonstrate the population's will to survive.

The war is over: Hitler's balcony on the Reich Chancellery in the summer of 1945.

The Berlin population soon realised that the anti-Hitler coalition would collapse. When the first US Army unit entered Berlin on 1st July to take over the American Sector as agreed, the soldiers had to spend the night under canvas in the Grunewald because their quarters were apparently still not available. In the summer of 1945, the Cold War had already cast its shadow.

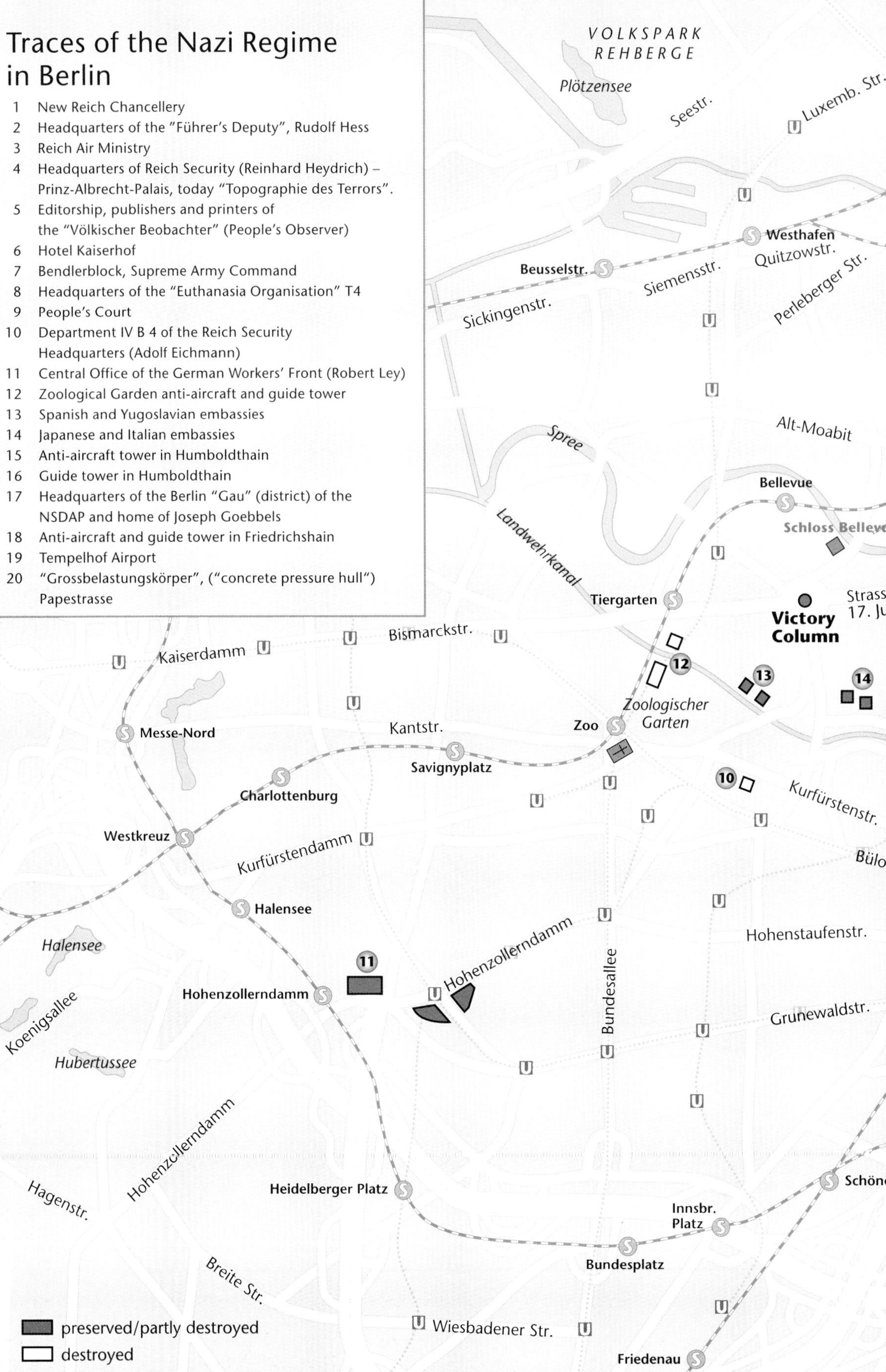
Traces of the Nazi Regime in Berlin
1 New Reich Chancellery
2 Headquarters of the "Führer's Deputy", Rudolf Hess
3 Reich Air Ministry
4 Headquarters of Reich Security (Reinhard Heydrich) – Prinz-Albrecht-Palais, today "Topographie des Terrors".
5 Editorship, publishers and printers of the "Völkischer Beobachter" (People's Observer)
6 Hotel Kaiserhof
7 Bendlerblock, Supreme Army Command
8 Headquarters of the "Euthanasia Organisation" T4
9 People's Court
10 Department IV B 4 of the Reich Security Headquarters (Adolf Eichmann)
11 Central Office of the German Workers' Front (Robert Ley)
12 Zoological Garden anti-aircraft and guide tower
13 Spanish and Yugoslavian embassies
14 Japanese and Italian embassies
15 Anti-aircraft tower in Humboldthain
16 Guide tower in Humboldthain
17 Headquarters of the Berlin "Gau" (district) of the NSDAP and home of Joseph Goebbels
18 Anti-aircraft and guide tower in Friedrichshain
19 Tempelhof Airport
20 "Grossbelastungskörper", ("concrete pressure hull") Papestrasse
VOLKSPARK REHBERGE
Plötzensee
Seestr.
Luxemb. Str.
Westhafen
Quitzowstr.
Beusselstr.
Siemensstr.
Perleberger Str.
Sickingenstr.
Spree
Alt-Moabit
Bellevue
Schloss Bellevue
Landwehrkanal
Tiergarten
Strasse 17. Jun
Victory Column
Kaiserdamm
Bismarckstr.
12
13
14
Zoologischer Garten
Zoo
Messe-Nord
Kantstr.
Savignyplatz
Charlottenburg
10
Kurfürstenstr.
Westkreuz
Kurfürstendamm
Bülow
Halensee
Hohenstaufenstr.
Halensee
11
Hohenzollerndamm
Hohenzollerndamm
Bundesallee
Grunewaldstr.
Koenigsallee
Hubertussee
Hohenzollerndamm
Hagenstr.
Heidelberger Platz
Schöne
Innsbr. Platz
Bundesplatz
Breite Str.
preserved/partly destroyed
destroyed
Wiesbadener Str.
Friedenau

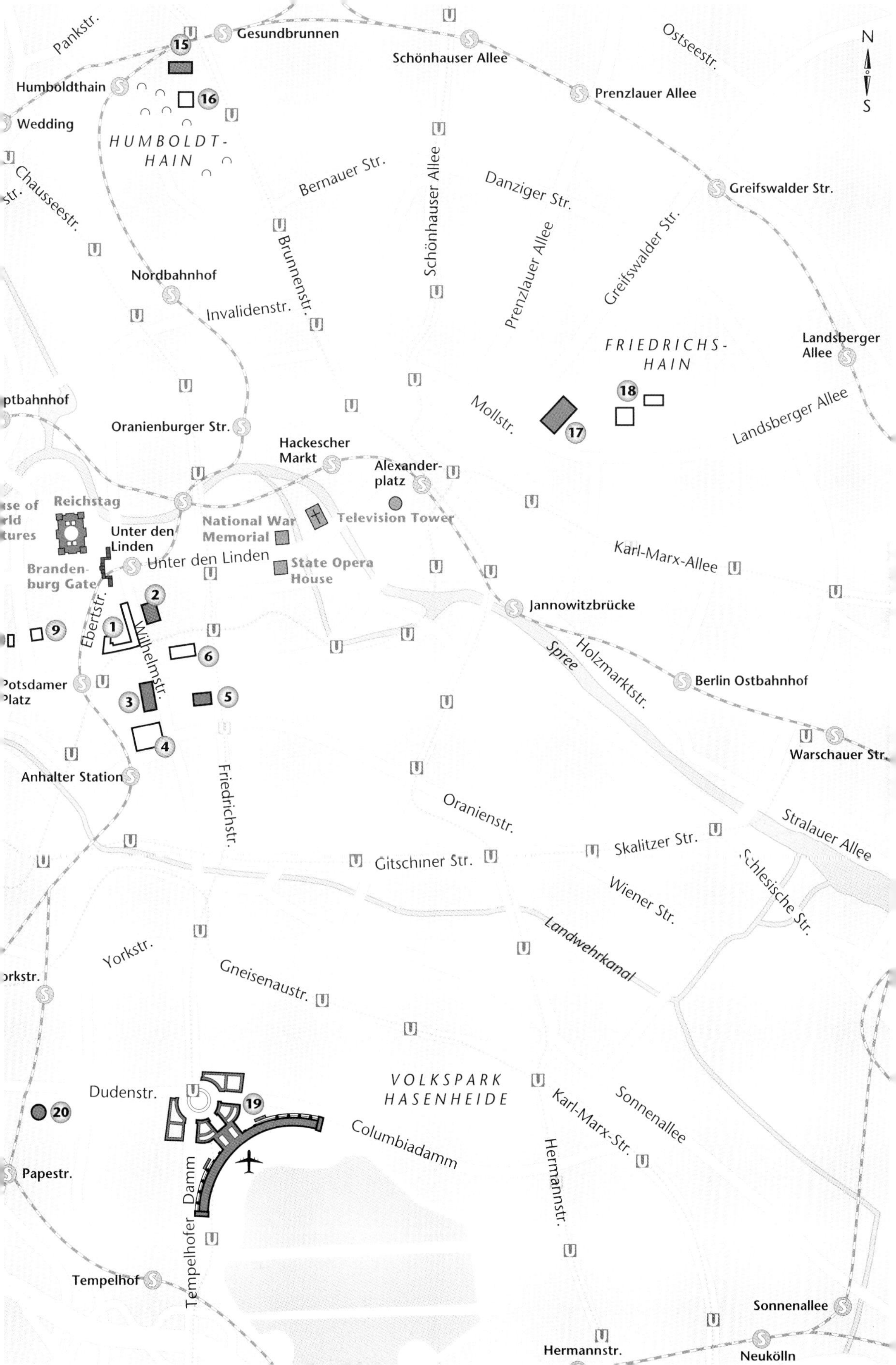
N
S
Pankstr.
Gesundbrunnen
Schönhauser Allee
Ostseestr.
Prenzlauer Allee
Humboldthain
Wedding
HUMBOLDT-HAIN
Chausseestr.
Bernauer Str.
Schönhauser Allee
Danziger Str.
Greifswalder Str.
Prenzlauer Allee
Greifswalder Str.
Brunnenstr.
Nordbahnhof
Invalidenstr.
FRIEDRICHS-HAIN
Landsberger Allee
Landsberger Allee
Mollstr.
Oranienburger Str.
Hackescher Markt
Alexanderplatz
Reichstag
National War Memorial
Television Tower
Unter den Linden
Unter den Linden
State Opera House
Brandenburg Gate
Karl-Marx-Allee
Jannowitzbrücke
Ebertstr.
Wilhelmstr.
Spree
Holzmarktstr.
Berlin Ostbahnhof
Warschauer Str.
Anhalter Station
Friedrichstr.
Oranienstr.
Stralauer Allee
Skalitzer Str.
Gitschiner Str.
Schlesische Str.
Wiener Str.
Landwehrkanal
Yorkstr.
Gneisenaustr.
VOLKSPARK HASENHEIDE
Dudenstr.
Karl-Marx-Str.
Sonnenallee
Columbiadamm
Hermannstr.
Papestr.
Tempelhofer Damm
Tempelhof
Sonnenallee
Hermannstr.
Neukölln

Nazi Addresses in Berlin
(Selection at end of 1939)

Institution	Address	Borough	Use today
Führer's (Reich) Chancellery	1, Vossstrasse (formerly Borsig-Palais)	Mitte	destroyed
Führer's Private Chancellery	55, Wilhelmstrasse	Mitte	destroyed
Seat of Deputy Führer (Rudolf Hess)	64, Wilhelmstrasse	Mitte	Federal Ministry for Agriculture
Reich Propaganda Ministry (extension building)	49, Wilhelmstrasse/ 45–32, Mauerstrasse	Mitte	Federal Ministry for Social Security
Federal Finance	97, Wilhelmstrasse	Mitte	Federal Finance Ministry
SS Reichsführer (Heinrich Himmler)	9, Prinz-Albrecht-Strasse (formerly Hotel Prinz Albrecht)	Kreuzberg	destroyed
Reich Press Chief of the NSDAP (Otto Dietrich)	63, Wilhelmstrasse	Mitte	destroyed
Leader of Reich Propaganda (Joseph Goebbels)	38, Belle-Alliance-Strasse (today Mehringdamm)	Kreuzberg	destroyed
Headquarters of the Berlin "Gau" (district) of the NSDAP (Joseph Goebbels)	22, Am Friedrichshain	Friedrichshain	Publishing house
General Inspectorate of Buldings (Albert Speer)	4, Pariser Platz	Mitte	Mostly destroyed; remainder part of the new Academy of Arts
Central Office of the German Workers' Front (Robert Ley)	Area around Fehrbelliner Platz	Wilmersdorf	Wilmersdorf Town Hall, Senate Administration, Federal Institute for Employees
Directorate of the Reich Employment Office (Konstantin Hierl)	1, Bismarckplatz	Wilmersdorf	Federal Office for the Environment
Head Office for the building of the Reich motorways	188–190, Potsdamer Strasse	Schöneberg	Head Office of the BVG (Berlin Transport)

Institution	Address	Borough	Use today
Chief of the Reich Security Office and the SD (Reinhard Heydrich)	102, Wilhelmstrasse (Prinz-Albrecht-Palais)	Kreuzberg	destroyed; today memorial site „Topographie des Terrors“
Central Office of the Secret State Police (Gestapo)	8, Prinz-Albrecht-Strasse	Kreuzberg	destroyed
Finance and Adminitration Office of the SS	129–135, Unter den Eichen	Steglitz	Office building
Head Office for Race and Settlement (SS)	22–24, Hedemannstrasse	Kreuzberg	destroyed
SS Head Office	100, Wilhelmstrasse	Kreuzberg	destroyed
Security Service of the SS (SD)	101, 103–104, 106, Wilhelmstrasse	Kreuzberg	destroyed
Department IV B 4 of the Reich Security Headquarters (Adolf Eichmann)	115–116, Kurfürstenstrasse	Tiergarten	destroyed
Head Office of the Euthanasia Organisation “T4”	4, Tiergartenstrasse	Tiergarten	destroyed
People’s Court	15, Bellevuestrasse	Tiergarten	destroyed
Editorship, publishers and printers of the Nazi newspapers, the “Völkischer Beobachter” (People’s Observer) and “Der Angriff” (The Attack)	88–91, Zimmerstrasse	Mitte	Partly destroyed, partly in use as a gallery and office building
Barracks of the SS “bodyguard (Leibstandarte) for Adolf Hitler”	63, Finckensteinallee	Steglitz	Federal Archieves
The Preussenhaus Foundation (containing numerous NSDAP institutions)	3–4, Leipziger Strasse	Mitte	Bundesrat (Federal Upper Chamber)
“Haus der Flieger”–Airmen House	5, Prinz-Albrecht-Strasse	Mitte	Berlin Members of Parliament building
SA Directorate, Berlin-Brandenburg	28, Kleine Alexanderstrasse	Mitte	Party Headquarters of the party DIE LINKE

Sources

Andreas-Friedrich, Ruth: Der Schattenmann. Tagebuchaufzeichnungen 1938-45. Frankfurt/M. 1986.

Boberach, Heinz (Hrsg.): Meldungen aus dem Reich. Auswahl aus den geheimen Lageberichten des Sicherheitsdienstes der SS 1939-1944. 17 Bde. und Registerband. Neuausgabe Herrsching 1984.

Dülffer, Jost/Thies, Jochen/Henke, Josef (Hrsg.): Hitlers Städte. Baupolitik im Dritten Reich. Köln – Wien 1978.

Engelbrechten, Julek [Julius] Karl von/Volz, Hans: Wir wandern durch das nationalsozialistische Berlin. Ein Führer durch die Gedenkstätten des Kampfes um die Reichshauptstadt. München 1937.

François-Poncet, André: Als Botschafter in Berlin. Mainz 1949.

Goebbels, Joseph: Kampf um Berlin. Bd. 1: Der Anfang 1926/27. 9. Aufl. München 1936.

Ders.: Die Tagebücher von Joseph Goebbels. Teil I. Aufzeichnungen 1923-1941. Hrsg. von Elke Fröhlich. 9 Bde. München 1998-2005.

Ders.: Die Tagebücher von Joseph Goebbels. Teil II: Diktate 1941-1945. 15 Bde. Hrsg. von Elke Fröhlich. München 1993-1996.

Hanfstaengl, Ernst: Zwischen Braunem und Weissem Haus. Erinnerungen eines politischen Aussenseiters. 2. Aufl. München 1970.

Hitler, Adolf: Mein Kampf. 479.-483. Auflage München 1939.

Ders.: Monologe im Führerhauptquartier 1941-1944. Die Aufzeichnungen Heinrich Heims. Hrsg. von Werner Jochmann. Hamburg 1980.

Ders.: Sämtliche Aufzeichnungen 1905-1924. Hrsg. von Eberhard Jäckel und Axel Kuhn. Stuttgart 1980.

Junge, Traudl: Bis zur letzten Stunde. Hitlers Sekretärin erzählt ihr Leben. Unter Mitarbeit von Melissa Müller. München 2002.

Kardorff, Ursula von: Berliner Aufzeichnungen aus den Jahren 1942-1945. Neuausgabe München 1992.

Kellerhoff, Sven Felix/Giebel, Wieland (Hrsg.): Als die Tage zu Nächten wurden. Berliner Schicksale im Luftkrieg. Berlin 2003.

Kennan, George F.: Memoiren eines Diplomaten. 3. Aufl. Stuttgart 1968.

Schroeder, Christa: Er war mein Chef. Aus dem Nachlass der Sekretärin von Adolf Hitler. 3. Aufl. München – Wien 1999.

Shirer, William L.: This is Berlin. Rundfunkreportagen aus Deutschland 1939/40. Leipzig 1999.

Smith, Howard K.: Feind schreibt mit. Ein amerikanischer Korrespondent erlebt Nazi-Deutschland. Frankfurt/M. 1986.

»Sopade«. Deutschland-Berichte der Sozialdemokratischen Partei Deutschlands 1934-1940. 7 Bde. 9. Aufl. Frankfurt/M. 1989.

Speer, Albert: Erinnerungen. Berlin 1969.

Bibliography

Arnold, Dietmar/Janick, Reiner: Sirenen und gepackte Koffer. Bunkeralltag in Berlin. Berlin 2003.

Beevor, Anthony: Berlin 1945. Das Ende. München 2002.

Benz, Wolfgang (Hrsg.): Überleben im Dritten Reich. Juden im Untergrund und ihre Helfer. München 2003.

Cullen, Michael S.: Der Reichstag. Parlament. Denkmal. Symbol. Berlin 1995.

Demps, Laurenz: Die Luftangriffe auf Berlin. Ein dokumentarischer Bericht. In: Jahrbuch des Märkischen Museums 4 (1978), S. 27-68.

Ders.: Berlin-Wilhelmstrasse. Eine Topographie preussisch-deutscher Macht. Berlin 2000.

Donath, Matthias: Architektur in Berlin 1933-1945. Ein Stadtführer. Berlin 2004.

Engelmann, Bernt: Berlin. Eine Stadt wie keine andere. Göttingen 1991.

Fest, Joachim: Hitler. Eine Biographie. Berlin – Frankfurt/M. 1973.

Girbig, Werner: ... im Anflug auf die Reichshauptstadt. Die Dokumentation der Bombenangriffe auf Berlin. Stuttgart 1970.

Gruner, Wolf: Judenverfolgung in Berlin 1933-1945. Eine Chronologie der Behördenmassnahmen in der Reichshauptstadt. Berlin 1996.

Ders.: Widerstand in der Rosenstrasse. Frankfurt/M. 2005.

Keil, Lars-Broder/Kellerhoff, Sven Felix: Deutsche Legenden. Vom Dolchstoss und anderen Mythen der Geschichte. 2. Aufl. Berlin 2003.

Dies.: Gerüchte machen Geschichte. Folgenreiche Falschmeldungen im 20. Jahrhundert. Berlin 2006.

Kellerhoff, Sven Felix: Mythos Führerbunker. Hitlers letzter Unterschlupf. Berlin 2003.

Ders.: Hitlers Berlin. Geschichte einer Hassliebe. Berlin 2005.

Kershaw, Ian: Hitler. 2 Bde. München 1998-2000.

Knobloch, Heinz: Der beherzte Reviervorsteher. Ungewöhnliche Zivilcourage am Hackeschen Markt. Neuausgabe Berlin 2003.

Kopleck, Mike: Berlin 1933-1945. Pastfinder. Stadtführer zu den Spuren der Vergangenheit. Berlin 2004.

Reichhardt, Hans J./Schäche, Wolfgang: Von Berlin nach Germania. Über die Zerstörungen der »Reichshauptstadt« durch Albert Speers Neugestaltungspläne. Neuausgabe Berlin 1998.

Reuth, Ralf Georg: Goebbels. München 1990.

Ribbe, Wolfgang (Hrsg.): Geschichte Berlins. 2 Bde. München 1987.

Rürup, Reinhard (Hrsg.): Topographie des Terrors. Gestapo, SS und Reichssicherheitshauptamt auf dem »Prinz-Albrecht-Gelände«. Eine Dokumentation. Berlin 1987.

Ders. (Hrsg.): 1936. Die Olympischen Spiele und der Nationalsozialismus. Eine Dokumentation. Berlin 1996.

Sandner, Harald: Wo war Hitler? Manuskript (unpublished).

Schäche, Wolfgang: Architektur und Städtebau in Berlin zwischen 1933 und 1945. 2. Aufl. Berlin 1992.
Ders./Szymanski, Norbert: Das Reichssportfeld. Architektur im Spannungsfeld von Sport und Macht. Berlin 2001.
Schoeps, Julius H. (Hrsg.): Berlin. Geschichte einer Stadt. Berlin 2001.
Tobias, Fritz: Der Reichstagsbrand. Legende und Wirklichkeit. Rastatt 1962.
Tuchel, Johannes/Schattenfroh, Reinold: Zentrale des Terrors. Prinz-Albrecht-Strasse 8: Hauptquartier der Gestapo. Berlin 1987.
Wilderotter, Hans: Alltag der Macht. Berlin Wilhelmstrasse. Berlin 1998.
Willems, Susanne: Der entsiedelte Jude. Albert Speers Wohnungsmarktpolitik für den Berliner Hauptstadtneubau. Berlin 2002.

The Author

Sven Felix Kellerhof, born in 1971 in Stuttgart, studied History and Media Law and graduated from the Berlin School of Journalism. Since 1993 he has been active as a publicist mainly for historical topics. He is currently Editor for Contemporary and Cultural History with the WELT.